Oxford AQA GCSE History (9-1)

C000321181

Norman England

c1066-c1100

Revision Guide

 RECAP   APPLY   REVIEW   SUCCEED

UPDATED

Changes to the AQA GCSE History specification 8145 (Version 1.3) and support for these changes

AQA released Version 1.3 of their AQA GCSE History specification in September 2019. The changes are to the command words and stems to a number of the AQA GCSE History questions to make the demands of the questions clearer for all students. Please refer to the AQA website for more information.

To support you with these changes, we have reviewed the content of this book and made the necessary small amends.

SERIES EDITOR

Tim Williams   **Aaron Wilkes**

OXFORD

Great Clarendon Street, Oxford, OX2 6DP, United Kingdom

Oxford University Press is a department of the University of Oxford.

It furthers the University's objective of excellence in research, scholarship, and education by publishing worldwide. Oxford is a registered trade mark of Oxford University Press in the UK and in certain other countries.

First published in 2018

Revised impression 2020

British Library Cataloguing in Publication Data

Data available

978-0-19-843284-5

Digital edition 978-0-19-843285-2

9 10 8

The manufacturing process conforms to the environmental regulations of the country of origin.

Printed in Great Britain by Bell and Bain Ltd. Glasgow

Acknowledgements

Cover: Universal History Archive/Getty Images

Artworks: QBS Learning

The publisher would like to thank Jon Cloake for his work on the Student Book on which this Revision Guide is based, and Laura Kibble for reviewing this Revision Guide.

We are grateful to the following for permission to include copyright material:

Daily Echo: 'How much has changed for Hampshire since Battle of Hastings?', *Southern Daily Echo*, 16 Oct 2016, used by permission of the Daily Echo.

Richard Huscroft: *Ruling England 1042–1217* (2e, Routledge, 2016), used by permission of the publishers, Taylor & Francis Group.

Marc Morris: 'Where History Happened: Norman Churches', *BBC History Magazine*, April 2013, copyright © BBC History/Immediate Media 2013, used by permission of Immediate Media Company London Ltd.

Peter Rex: *1066: A New History of the Norman Conquest* (Amberley, 2011), used by permission of Amberley Publishing.

Ed West: 'The Normans were the original liberal metropolitan elite 'Remainers'', *The Spectator*, 14 Oct 2016, used by permission of The Spectator.

We have made every effort to trace and contact all copyright holders before publication. If notified of any errors or omissions, the publisher will be happy to rectify these at the earliest opportunity.

Links to third party websites are provided by Oxford in good faith and for information only. Oxford disclaims any responsibility for the materials contained in any third party website referenced in this work.

From the author, Tim Williams: I would like to thank Aaron Wilkes, Jon Cloake, Rebecca DeLozier, Janice Chan, Tamsin Shelton and all at OUP for their hard work, support and guidance. Thank you, as always, to my incredibly supportive family.

Contents

RECAP APPLY REVIEW

Part one:
The Normans: conquest and control

Part two:
Life under the Normans

Contents

Part three:

The Norman Church and monasticism

Introduction

The *Oxford AQA GCSE History* textbook series has been developed by an expert team led by Jon Cloake and Aaron Wilkes. This matching revision guide offers you step-by-step strategies to master your AQA Depth Study: Norman England exam skills, and the structured revision approach of **Recap, Apply** and **Review** to prepare you for exam success.

Use the **Checklists** on pages 3–4 to keep track of your revision, and use the traffic light feature on each page to monitor your confidence level on each topic. Other exam practice and revision features include **Top Revision Tips** on page 6, and the **'How to...'** guides for each exam question type on pages 7–9.

RECAP Each chapter recaps key events and developments through easy-to-digest chunks and visual diagrams. **Key terms** appear in bold and red; they are defined in the glossary. indicates the relevant Oxford AQA History Student Book pages so you can easily reread the textbook for further revision.

SUMMARY highlights the most important facts at the end of each chapter.

TIMELINE provides a short list of dates to help you remember key events.

APPLY Each revision activity is designed to help drill your understanding of facts, and then progress towards applying your knowledge to exam questions.

These targeted revision activities are written specifically for this guide, which will help you apply your knowledge towards the four exam questions in your AQA Norman England exam paper:

INTERPRETATION ANALYSIS **EXPLAIN** **WRITE AN ACCOUNT** **HISTORIC ENVIRONMENT**

 Examiner Tip highlights key parts of an exam question, and gives you hints on how to avoid common mistakes in exams.

 Revision Skills provides different revision techniques. Research shows that using a variety of revision styles can help cement your revision.

 Review gives you helpful reminders about how to check your answers and how to revise further.

REVIEW Throughout each chapter, you can review and reflect on the work you have done, and find advice on how to further refresh your knowledge.

You can tick off the Review column from the progress checklist as you work through this revision guide. The **Activity Answers Guidance** and the **Exam Practice** sections with full sample student answers also help you to review your own work.

Top revision tips

Getting your revision right

It is perfectly natural to feel anxious when exam time approaches. The best way to keep on top of the stress is to be organised!

3 months to go

Plan: create a realistic revision timetable, and stick to it!

Track your progress: use the Progress Checklists (pages 3–4) to help you track your revision. It will help you stick to your revision plan.

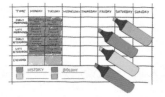

Be realistic: revise in regular, small chunks, of around 30 minutes. Reward yourself with 10 minute breaks — you will be amazed how much more you'll remember.

Positive thinking: motivate yourself by turning your negative thoughts to positive ones. Instead of asking *'why can't I remember this topic at all?'* ask yourself *'what different techniques can I try to improve my memory?'*

Organise: make sure you have everything you need — your revision books, coloured pens, index cards, sticky notes, paper, etc. Find a quiet place where you are comfortable. Divide your notes into sections that are easy to use.

Timeline: create a timeline with colour-coded sticky notes, to make sure you remember important dates relating to the three parts of the Norman British Depth Study (use the Timeline on page 11 as a starting point).

Practise: ask your teachers for practice questions or past papers.

Revision techniques

Using a variety of revision techniques can help you remember information, so try out different methods:

- Make **flashcards**, using both sides of the card to test yourself on key figures, dates, and definitions

- **Colour-code** your notebooks
- **Reread** your textbook or copy out your notes
- Create **mind-maps** for complicated topics

- Draw **pictures** and symbols that spring to mind
- **Group study:** find a **buddy** or group to revise with and test you

- Listen to revision **podcasts** or watch revision **clips**
- Work through the **revision activities** in this guide.

Revision tips to help you pass your Norman England exam

1 month to go

Key concepts: make sure you understand key concepts for this topic, such as conquest, feudalism, patronage and monasticism. If you're unsure, attend revision sessions and ask your teacher.

Identify your weaknesses: which topics or question types are easier and which are more challenging for you? Schedule more time to revise the challenging topics or question types.

Make it stick: find memorable ways to remember chronology, using fun rhymes, or doodles, for example.

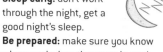

Take a break: do something completely different during breaks — listen to music, take a short walk, make a cup of tea, for example.

Check your answers: answer the exam questions in this guide, *then* check the Activity answers guidance at the end of the guide to practise applying your knowledge to exam questions.

Understand your mark scheme: review the Mark scheme (page 10) for each exam question, and make sure you understand how you will be marked.

Master your exam skills: study and remember the How to master your exam skills steps (pages 7–9) for each AQA question type — it will help you plan your answers quickly!

Time yourself: practise making plans and answering exam questions within the recommended time limits.

Take mock exams seriously: you can learn from them how to manage your time better under exam conditions.

Rest well: make sure your phone and laptop are put away at least an hour before bed. This will help you rest better.

On the big day

Sleep early: don't work through the night, get a good night's sleep.

Be prepared: make sure you know where and when the exam is, and leave plenty of time to get there.

Check: make sure you have all your equipment in advance, including spare pens!

Drink and eat healthily: avoid too much caffeine or junk food. Water is best — if you are 5% dehydrated, then your concentration drops 20%.

Stay focused: don't listen to people who might try to wind you up about what might come up in the exam — they don't know any more than you.

Good luck!

Master your exam skills

Get to grips with your Paper 2: Norman England British Depth Study

The Paper 2 exam lasts 2 hours, and you have to answer eight questions covering two topics. The first four questions (worth 40 marks) will cover your Thematic Study topic; the last four questions (40 marks) will cover Norman England. Here, you will find details about what to expect from the last four questions which relate to the British Depth Study topic Norman England, and advice on how to master your exam skills.

You should spend about 50 minutes in total on the Norman England questions – see pages 8–9 for how long to spend on each question.

The four questions will always follow this pattern:

▼ INTERPRETATION A

1   How convincing is **Interpretation A** about…? Explain your answer based on your contextual knowledge and what it says in **Interpretation A**.

8 marks

2   Explain what was important about…

8 marks

3   Write an account of…

8 marks

4   How far does a study of… support this statement? Explain your answer. You should refer to… and your contextual knowledge.

16 marks

REVISION SKILLS

Read the *Thematic Study Revision Guide* for help on the first four questions of Paper 2.

EXAMINER TIP

For this question, you need to focus on the content of the interpretation and how it fits within your contextual knowledge.

EXAMINER TIP

You will already know what the historic environment site is for your exam. Make sure you are confident in explaining its features and how they relate to the historical context of Norman England.

EXAMINER TIP

This question is worth a lot of marks and requires a longer answer. Make sure you leave plenty of time to complete it at the end of the exam.

REVIEW

If you find interpretations challenging, look out for the INTERPRETATION ANALYSIS activities throughout this guide to help you revise and drill your understanding of the 'interpretation' questions. Look out for the REVISION SKILLS tips too, to inspire you to find the revision strategies that work for you!

How to master the 'interpretation' question

Here are the steps to consider when answering the 'interpretation' question. Remember that this question is similar to the third 'interpretation' question in Paper 1, but this focuses on one interpretation only.

Question 1

- **Content:** Read through the interpretation carefully. What point is the writer making about the subject? Underline any key points or arguments that are made.

- **Context:** Now think back over your own knowledge. Does the content of the interpretation fit with what you know? Does it give a fair reflection of the person, event or issue it describes? Are its conclusions reasonable?

- **Conclude:** You now need to make a judgement about the interpretation. Do you find it convincing as an assessment of the person, event or issue it describes? Make sure you refer to the content of the interpretation and your own, relevant contextual knowledge in your answer.

- ⏱ Spend about 10 minutes on this 8-mark question.

How to master the 'explain' question

Here are the steps to consider when answering the 'explain' question. You may be asked to consider the importance of a key event/feature/person relating to cause and consequence ('why did it happen?' and 'what happened as a result?') or change and continuity ('what is different?' and 'what stayed the same?').

Question 2

- **Plan:** Think back over your knowledge of the topic referred to in the question to plan your answer. This question requires you to show strong knowledge and understanding of the event or issue stated.

- **Importance:** You need to say what made the event/feature/person *important*. In what ways did it have an impact on the wider historical period? Did it affect people's lives? Did it have an impact on politics or the government? Did it lead to change? What happened as a result?

- ⏱ Spend around 10 minutes on this 8-mark question.

EXAMINER TIP

You should aim to include 3–4 reasons or facts that made the event or issue important. Make sure you explain them and include historical detail to support your points.

How to master the 'write an account' question

Here are the steps to consider when answering the 'write an account' question. This question involves telling the key moments of an event in relation to the topic of the question. You need to describe, explain and analyse how one development led to another.

Question 3

- **Select the key moments:** What will you include in your story? Spend 1 minute to work out 3–4 key moments that are *relevant* to the question. Make sure you organise the moments in chronological order (starting with the earliest). You must include 1–2 specific historical facts for each key moment and plenty of specific historical detail.

- **Link your story:** Write your answer based on the key moments you have identified, and explain *how* the moments link together to cause the event to develop. Make sure you link your answer to the point of the question. A top-level answer will also include an explanation of the consequences of the events on the wider historical period of Norman England.

- ⏱ You should spend about 10 minutes on this 8-mark question.

EXAMINER TIP

Use phrases like 'this led to …' and 'as a result of this …' to help you to structure your answer.

How to master the 'historic environment' question

The last question in Paper 2 will always relate to the historic environment. You have to show how your knowledge of the specific site helps you to understand the key features of Norman England. In other words, what can a study of the historic environment tell you about people or events at the time?

Question 4

- **Read the question carefully:** What statement is the question asking you to consider? The statement is located within the quotation marks. Underline key words in the statement to help you focus your answer.

- **Plan your essay:** Consider the questions below.

  o **Motivation:** Why was the site created?

  o **Location:** Why is it in this particular location?

  o **Function:** Why was it built in this specific way? Identify and explain specific building features, and the job they do.

  o **Purpose:** What was the building used for? Who lived or worked there? How is its purpose reflected in the design?

- If the site is a battle (such as the Battle of Hastings), you should consider instead: Why was the battle fought (**motivation**)? Why was it fought in that particular **location**? What happened at the battle?

- **Context:** Now that you have considered your specific historic site, you need to consider what it tells you about the Norman era. The question will guide you in this. You need to select *relevant* information about the motivation/location/function/purpose which reflects the aspect of the Norman era mentioned in the exam question (you should have underlined this aspect). Your answer needs to link your knowledge of the period with your knowledge of the site.

- **Conclude:** This question will ask you 'how far …' the historic site has helped you to back up a statement about Norman England, so make sure you come to a clear conclusion when you answer this question.

- ⏱ You should spend around 20 minutes on this 16-mark question.

REVIEW

You can find sample student answers to each question type in the Exam Practice pages at the end of this guide.

EXAMINER TIP

Don't forget you will also have to answer four questions relating to your Thematic Study in Paper 2. Ensure you leave enough time to complete both sections of Paper 2! You are advised to spend 50 minutes on your Thematic Study in the exam.

AQA GCSE History mark schemes

Below are simplified versions of the AQA mark schemes, to help you understand the marking criteria for your **Paper 2: Norman England** exam.

Level	'Interpretation' question
4	• Complex evaluation of the interpretation. • Argument about how convincing the interpretation is, is shown throughout the answer, supported by relevant facts/understanding. *7–8 marks*
3	• Developed evaluation of the interpretation referring to at least two aspects of the interpretation. • Argument is stated about how convincing the interpretation is. Answer is supported by relevant facts/understanding. *5–6 marks*
2	• Simple answer referring to one aspect of the interpretation. • Answer is supported with relevant facts/understanding. *3–4 marks*
1	• Basic answer on the interpretation. • Some facts/understanding are shown. *1–2 marks*

Level	'Explain' question
4	• Complex explanation of several consequences/causes/changes. • A range of accurate, detailed and relevant facts are shown. *7–8 marks*
3	• Developed explanation of two or more consequences/causes/changes. • A range of accurate, relevant facts are shown. *5–6 marks*
2	• Simple explanation of one consequence/cause/change. • Specific relevant facts are shown. *3–4 marks*
1	• Basic explanation of consequences/causes/changes. • Some basic related facts are shown. *1–2 marks*

Level	'Write an account' question
4	• Complex analysis of consequences/causes/changes. • A carefully selected story with a range of accurate and relevant facts is shown. *7–8 marks*
3	• Developed analysis of consequence/cause/change. • Structured and well-ordered story with a range of accurate and relevant facts is shown. *5–6 marks*
2	• Simple analysis of consequence/cause/change. • Structured story with specific relevant facts is shown. *3–4 marks*
1	• Basic analysis of consequence/cause/change. • Straightforward story with some basic related facts is shown. *1–2 marks*

Level	'Historic environment' question
4	• Complex explanation of consequences/causes/changes. • Argument is shown throughout the structured answer, supported by a range of accurate, detailed and relevant facts about the site and the wider historical period. *13–16 marks*
3	• Developed explanation of changes. • Argument is shown throughout the structured answer, supported by a range of accurate and relevant facts about the site. *9–12 marks*
2	• Simple explanation of changes. • Argument is shown, supported by specific, relevant facts about the site. *5–8 marks*
1	• Basic explanation of changes. • Some basic related facts about the site are shown. *1–4 marks*

Norman England 1066–c1100 Timeline

The colours and symbols represent different types of event as follows:

Red: political events   Blue: battles

Green: rebellions and the response to rebellions   Yellow: religious events

1066   **January** – King Edward the Confessor dies; Harold Godwinson crowned King of England

1066   **September** – Battle of Fulford Gate; Battle of Stamford Bridge

October – Battle of Hastings

1066   **December** – William crowned King of England

1069   The Harrying of the North

1070   Lanfranc becomes Archbishop of Canterbury

1071   The East Anglia Rebellion, led by Hereward the Wake

1075   The revolt of the Norman earls

1078-1122   The Investiture Controversy

1086   The Domesday Survey is completed

1087   Death of King William I. Robert Curthose becomes Duke of Normandy and William II (Rufus) becomes King of England

1089   Anselm becomes Archbishop of Canterbury

1093   The construction of Durham Cathedral begins

1100   Death of William II

CHAPTER 1

Causes of the Norman Conquest

England before 1066

Government

- Ruled by King Edward the Confessor since 1042. The calm and order of Edward's rule followed a time of instability.
- The country was divided into earldoms. **Earls** could become very powerful and needed to be well managed by the king to maintain order.

Population

- The population was around 2 million, with the majority living in the southern part of the country.

Society

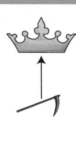

- There was a clear hierarchy in Anglo-Saxon society. The king was at the top, followed by the earls and the **clergy**. The peasants were at the bottom.

England before 1066

Defence

- The king and the earls commanded 2500–3000 professional soldiers known as **housecarls**. They also had the right to call upon the peasants to fight for them in times of need.

Religion

- Religion was central to the lives of Anglo-Saxons and the Catholic Church was very powerful. Led by the Pope in Rome but controlled in England by bishops and other members of the clergy, the Church owned large amounts of land and made rules on everything from marriage to inheritance.

Wealth

- England was wealthy and was a target for foreign raiders like Vikings. This put coastal areas, particularly in the north, at risk.
- Trade, notably with France and Scandinavia, allowed England to add to its wealth.
- It had one of the most advanced economic systems in the world with its own **minting** system for producing coins and a treasury that co-ordinated taxation and spending by the government.

The power of the Godwins

Other than the king, the most powerful man in England was Godwin, Earl of Wessex. Godwin and his family controlled the largest and most important earldom in the country, stretching from Cornwall in the south-west to Norfolk in the east, but also commanded huge support among the people. Unlike Edward, Godwin was a respected military leader. Over time, the family's power increased further with the marriage of Godwin's daughter, Edith, to the king and the appointment of his sons, Sweyn, Harold and Tostig, to powerful positions. After a public falling out in 1052, Edward exiled the family but less than a year later they returned with a large army. The king was unable to raise an opposition force and simply had to accept Godwin's return. Historians disagree about the level of influence Godwin and his sons actually had, but there is no doubt that they were a force to be reckoned with in England.

▲ The map shows the English earldoms in 1066; borders often changed according to who was earl and how much power they had; the king could take land away or give land as a reward, depending upon the relationship he had with the earl

 APPLY

WRITE AN ACCOUNT

a Create your own illustrated version of the spider diagram to show what England was like in 1066.

b Write a 100-word summary of England before the Norman invasion.

REVISION SKILLS

Writing short summaries is a good way of ensuring you have a clear understanding of a topic.

EXPLAIN

a Who were the Godwins?

b Write a paragraph to answer the question: 'Why were the Godwins powerful?'

EXAMINER TIP

Although the topic starts in 1066, it is important to understand the situation before Edward's death. Make sure you are able to explain who Harold Godwinson was and why he was such a powerful figure.

The death of Edward the Confessor

When Edward the Confessor died childless on 5 January 1066, he left the kingdom without an obvious ruler. There were no official rules of succession in Anglo-Saxon England. A claim to the throne could be made in several ways:

- The king's son (generally the eldest) would have the strongest claim.
- Another male relative, for example the king's brother, might have a reasonable claim.
- A male relative of a previous king could make a claim.
- The king could name a successor to take over when he died (*post obitum*). If this was on his deathbed, it was known as *novissima verba*.

- The **Witan** (the leading earls and clergy) could nominate the successor.
- Claimants could use force to take the throne.

The four claimants

There were four main claimants to the throne in January 1066:

- Harold Godwinson
- Edgar the Aetheling
- William, Duke of Normandy
- Harald Hardrada.

Harold Godwinson, Earl of Wessex (1022–1066)

- Following the death of his father, Earl Godwin, Harold had become an extremely important figure in Edward's government. He became 'sub-regulus', acting as a 'deputy king', from 1060 onwards. He was also Edward's brother-in-law.
- He had shown loyalty to Edward, even over his own brother Tostig.
- Harold claimed that Edward had promised him the throne on his deathbed.
- He had the support of the English nobles and the Witan.
- He had himself crowned king on 6 January, the same day as Edward's funeral.

Edgar the Aetheling (c1051–1126)

- Edgar was the great-nephew of Edward the Confessor, and therefore a blood relation (**aetheling** means 'prince').
- Edgar had lived with King Edward since childhood and was treated by many as his adopted son.
- As an Anglo-Saxon, Edgar had the support of many English earls.
- As he was only a teenager in 1066, Edgar lacked the experience and political and military skill to challenge Harold Godwinson's coronation.

⚙ APPLY

EXPLAIN

a Create a spider diagram to show the basis on which someone could make a claim to the throne.

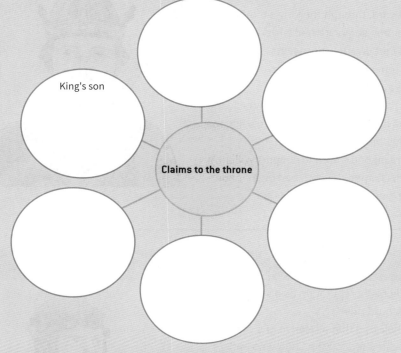

King's son

Claims to the throne

b Harold Godwinson and Edgar the Aetheling were the two English claimants. Complete the table below to show whose claim was the strongest:

Arguments in favour of Harold Godwinson	Arguments in favour of Edgar the Aetheling

c **EXAM QUESTION** Explain what was important about Harold Godwinson's claim to the throne.

EXAMINER TIP 🎯

For this question you need to consider how far Harold met the criteria listed on the page opposite. For example, he could make his claim as a nominated successor of Edward but he was not a blood relation to a previous king.

WRITE AN ACCOUNT

a Create a fact file for Harold Godwinson. You may want to use the information on the page opposite to add additional background detail.

b Write a summary of why Harold Godwinson believed he should be king.

REVISION SKILLS

Focusing on key individuals can be a good way of revising the period. Start with someone's name or picture (e.g. Harold Godwinson) and then surround it with information about who they were and how they connect to wider events.

William, Duke of Normandy (c1028–1087)

- A successful but ruthless military leader, William had been Duke of Normandy since the age of seven.
- He was a distant cousin of King Edward, through the king's mother, Emma of Normandy. There is also some suggestion of a friendship between them, although they only met on a few occasions.
- William claimed that Edward had promised him the throne when William had visited England several years before.
- Edward had grown up in Normandy and his court and rule were clearly influenced by this. Some historians have argued that Edward's actions as king suggest that he wanted a Norman to succeed him.
- William claimed that Harold Godwinson had sworn to support William's claim to the throne in 1064. William claimed the oath had been made over a holy relic and was therefore binding in the eyes of God.

Harald Hardrada (1015–1066)

- As the Viking king of Norway, Harald had a reputation as a strong and powerful warrior (Hardrada means 'hard ruler').
- As Edward had no sons, Hardrada believed that a relative of a previous king should take over. Hardrada was related to King Cnut, who had ruled England from 1016 to 1035. As a result, Hardrada thought he should be next to rule England.
- Harald claimed that his father, Magnus, had been promised the throne by Cnut's son Harthacnut. However, when Harthacnut died in 1042, it was Edward who took the throne. Magnus had since died, but his son was determined to claim what he thought was rightfully his.

SUMMARY

- England under Edward the Confessor was stable and prosperous.
- The Godwins were a powerful and influential family.
- Edward died childless in January 1066 and there were no firm rules of succession in place.
- There were a number of claimants for the throne:
  - o Harold Godwinson
  - o Edgar the Aetheling
  - o William, Duke of Normandy
  - o Harald Hardrada.
- Harold Godwinson was crowned king on 6 January 1066.

APPLY

EXPLAIN

a Remind yourself of the different criteria on which a claim to the throne could be made.

- The king's son (generally the eldest) would have the strongest claim.
- Another male relative, for example the king's brother, might have a reasonable claim.
- A male relative of a previous king could make a claim.
- The king could name a successor to take over when he died (*post obitum*). If this was on his deathbed, it was known as *novissima verba*.
- The Witan (the leading earls and clergy) could nominate the successor.
- Claimants could use force to take the throne.

For each claimant, create a flashcard. On one side write the claimant's name and on the other make a list of any of the criteria that they fit.

b Who do you think had the strongest claim? Why?

_____

_____

_____

INTERPRETATION ANALYSIS

Read the interpretation below:

▼ **INTERPRETATION A** *Adapted from* A Brief History of Britain, 1066–1485: The Birth of a Nation *by Nicholas Vincent (2011):*

> William's supporters wrote to back William's right to invade England with legal and religious reasons. Edward, they argued, had promised the throne to William long before 1066 (a claim for which there is no real proof). They also said that Harold had sworn a sacred oath on holy relics, promising to support Williams claim to be king of England.

a What does the interpretation suggest about William's claim to the throne? Does it suggest that his claim was justified?

_____

_____

_____

b
 How convincing is **Interpretation A** about William's claim to the throne in 1066? Explain your answer based on your contextual knowledge and what it says in **Interpretation A**.

EXAMINER TIP

For this question, you need to include your own knowledge about William's claim as well as what is included in the interpretation.

REVIEW

If you are unsure about how to analyse the interpretation, review the step-by-step guide on page 8 about how to master your interpretation analysis exam skills.

Norman England c1066–c1100 Revision Guide   17

CHAPTER 2

Military aspects

RECAP

William prepares to invade

The situation in France

- Although William's dukedom only covered the area of Normandy, he had conquered the neighbouring area of Maine in 1063.
- In 1066, the king of France was just 14 years old and did not present a serious threat to William's independence. This along with a civil war in Anjou meant that William was one of the most powerful men in north-western Europe. With no real threat nearby, the duke could look across the English Channel.

▲ Map showing Anglo-Saxon England, and areas of France controlled by William of Normandy, other dukes and the king of France

Getting across the Channel

- Keeping the men and the fleet in good condition was vital for William. He kept his men well fed but also insisted on total discipline. Punishments were brutal for those who stepped out of line.
- He stationed his fleet in Saint-Valery-sur-Somme on the mouth of the River Somme, moving it from further south and thereby cutting the distance to England down to just 33km (20 miles).

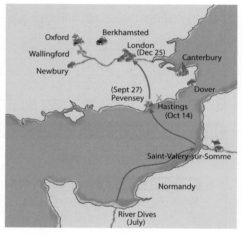

▲ Map showing the relocation of William's fleet

The support of God: the Papal Banner

- William was able to secure the support of the Pope for his invasion of England by persuading the Pope that as king he would be able to reform the English Catholic Church. Marching behind the **Papal Banner** helped him gain wider support for his invasion as people believed God was on his side.

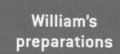

William's preparations

Military preparations: building an army

- As well as loyal Normans, William recruited men from across western Europe. Many were willing to fight beneath the Papal Banner in a **Holy War**, others were simply mercenaries, attracted by the promise of riches and land in England.
- A force of around 8000 was eventually assembled.

Military preparations: building a fleet and preparing to invade

- William spent a fortune building a large fleet in order to sail across the Channel.
- Flat-bottomed boats were built to make it easier to transport horses.
- New weapons were made and 'flat-pack' castles were prepared, ready to be put up as soon as the Normans secured land in England.

The Normans land in England

Despite William's thorough preparations, his invasion was delayed for six weeks because the wind was blowing in the wrong direction. Although frustrating at the time, the delay ultimately worked to William's advantage. When he arrived at Pevensey on 28 September 1066, the English coast was completely undefended. Having waited for weeks, Harold Godwinson had been forced to send his men home. Most were farmers, and it was harvest time so they were needed back in the fields.

 **APPLY**

WRITE AN ACCOUNT

a Create a set of flashcards showing William's preparations. On one side, write the title and on the other write an explanation.

b Use the following headings to categorise William's preparations:

- Military
- Political
- Religious.

c What links can you make between the preparations? Do any fit into more than one category?

d **EXAM QUESTION** Write an account of the preparations William made to invade England.

 EXAMINER TIP

For a 'write an account' question you need to describe the series of events and link them together to form a narrative. Remember to include specific detail.

EXPLAIN

a What was the Papal Banner and why was it important to William?

_____

_____

_____

b Can you make any links between the Papal Banner and the other preparations that William made? How important do you think it was?

_____

_____

_____

_____

_____

_____

REVISION SKILLS

Remember that the exam rewards you for accurate spelling, punctuation and grammar (SPaG) — make sure you get into good habits as you revise!

While Harold Godwinson was making the decision to disband his army in the south, another claimant to the throne, Harald Hardrada, made his move. Hardrada and his 300 Viking ships sailed up the River Humber and landed 16km (10 miles) from the city of York in the north. Supporters of Harold were ready to defend their land and the first battle of 1066 began.

The Battle of Fulford Gate

The first battle: Fulford Gate, 20 September 1066

- Hardrada and around 7000 Vikings were joined by Tostig Godwinson, Harold Godwinson's brother.
- The English were commanded by Harold's two brothers-in-law, Edwin, Earl of Mercia, and Morcar, Earl of Northumbria. The army consisted of around 3500 men.
- The initial English attack took the Vikings by surprise but Viking numbers overwhelmed the Anglo-Saxon army and Edwin and Morcar were defeated.
- Hardrada was victorious, the English army was scattered and the earls forced to flee. However, the Vikings had significant casualties.

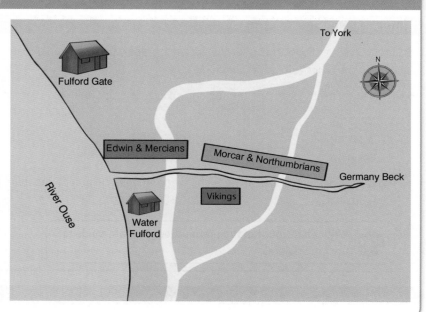

The Battle of Stamford Bridge

The second battle: Stamford Bridge, 25 September 1066

- The loss at Fulford Gate meant that Harold Godwinson had to move quickly. He reassembled his army and marched 306km (190 miles) in four days, gathering more troops as he went.
- The Anglo-Saxons reached Tadcaster, on the outskirts of York, on 24 September and the following morning they launched a surprise attack on the Viking camp.
- The battle was centred around the undefended Stamford Bridge and was a long and bloody one. The Vikings were scattered and not ready for battle but still fought hard. Hardrada and Tostig were both killed; Harold Godwinson had destroyed the Viking threat and removed a major rival to his throne.
- Harold's victory was a great one, but just three days later, word reached him that William's fleet had finally landed in the south.

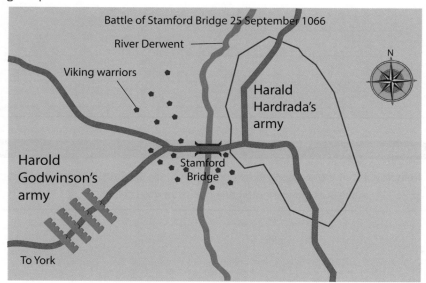

APPLY

WRITE AN ACCOUNT

a Create a storyboard that shows the events of Harald Hardrada's invasion. Include both battles.

b

> **EXAM QUESTION** Write an account of Harald Harada's invasion of England.

EXPLAIN

a Make a list of the key events that have taken place so far in 1066. Make sure you include the activities of all the main contenders for the throne.

b Put these events in chronological order, below, with the earliest at the top. Make sure you include dates where appropriate.

Events of 1066

c Colour code your chronological list using the following categories:

- Events involving William ☐
- Events involving Harold Godwinson ☐
- Events involving Harald Hardrada. ☐

Anglo-Saxon and Norman tactics

Preparing for the Battle of Hastings

King Harold and the Anglo-Saxons		Duke William and the Normans
	Army	
Around 7000 — mostly **fyrd**, with some **thegns**. Also elite housecarls, although many had been killed at Stamford Bridge. Survivors of the fight against the Vikings were exhausted having marched 300km (190 miles) south following Harold's decision to head straight into battle, rather than give his men time to rest.		Combination of soldiers from Normandy and mercenaries from other parts of France and western Europe, totalling approximately 7000 men. Highly skilled archers and cavalry (soldiers on horseback). Men were well rested having landed several days before. They had spent the time burning villages and building the first **motte** and **bailey** castle.
	Weaponry and armour	
Double-handed axes, pikes, large circular shields; housecarls had armour; peasants used pitchforks, farming equipment, and weapons and armour taken from fallen soldiers.		Bows, large tear-shaped shields that covered from chin to knee, pikes, armour.
	Battle tactics and strategy	
Shield wall — interlocking of shields to prevent an enemy advance. All soldiers on foot (infantry), including Harold.		Infantry and cavalry. Archers to wear down the enemy. The army organised into divisions and a flag system was used for communication to allow tactics to be changed during battle. William on horseback.
	Position on battlefield	
The top of Senlac Hill.		The base of Senlac Hill with marshy land either side.
	The leaders	
An experienced general who had successfully fought the Welsh and the Vikings. Many supporters in England, including most nobles and the Witan.		A highly experienced general. Conquered areas around Normandy and as far away as Sicily. Had the support of the Pope and the king of France, and was supported by or allied with the leaders of the states that bordered Normandy.

 **APPLY**

INTERPRETATION ANALYSIS

Read the interpretation below:

▼ **INTERPRETATION A** *Adapted from* 1066: A New History of the Norman Conquest *by Peter Rex (2011):*

> The real evidence for the size of the English army comes from Robert FitzWimarc, an Anglo-Saxon nobleman who sided with Duke William when he landed at Pevensey. FitzWimarc warned William that King Harold was on his way to confront him, with 'innumerable soldiers all well-equipped for war', and compared with Harold's army William had only 'a pack of curs'.* The fact that the Normans could not overcome English resistance after nearly nine hours of fierce fighting suggests that the two armies were almost evenly balanced.
>
> * A pack of curs = a pack of aggressive mongrel dogs. A cur can also mean a despicable or cowardly person. This could also be a reference to the mix of people that made up William's army.

a What does the interpretation suggest about:

- the Anglo-Saxon army
- the Norman army?

b What conclusion does the writer come to about the two sides?

c Does the conclusion fit with your knowledge of the two armies before the Battle of Hastings?

d

 EXAM QUESTION How convincing is **Interpretation A** about the two armies that fought at the Battle of Hastings? Explain your answer based on your contextual knowledge and what it says in **Interpretation A**.

EXAMINER TIP

The interpretation describes the armies as 'evenly balanced'. Make sure you use the information in the table above to help you decide whether or not this is a fair statement.

EXAMINER TIP

As you read an interpretation, highlight key words and sentences that tell you what the writer is arguing. Remember, it is still possible to know what an interpretation is arguing even if there are words or phrases that you don't understand.

EXPLAIN

a Complete the table below about the two armies before the battle:

Harold's advantages	William's advantages

b Who do you think had the biggest advantage before the battle? Explain your answer.

The Battle of Hastings

1

The battle began at 9am. The Anglo-Saxons formed their shield wall and the Normans were unable to break through. Norman arrows flew over the heads of the English frontline or hit the shields. Calvary charges proved useless against the firm Anglo-Saxon line.

2

After a number of failed attacks, one group of Normans ran back from the line. Sensing victory, a group of Anglo-Saxons gave chase, causing a break in the shield wall. But when they became trapped in the marshland, the Anglo-Saxons were slaughtered. William ordered more **feigned retreats** like this and finally the Anglo-Saxon line began to be worn down.

3

During a break in the battle to allow both sides to recover their dead and wounded, William changed tactics. He moved his archers to the front and ordered them to fire into the air. The arrows landed on top of the Anglo-Saxons, behind the shield wall, causing chaos.

4

Fearing the arrival of Anglo-Saxon reinforcements, William made one final push for victory. A combination of the feigned retreats, constant arrow fire and a full-scale cavalry attack meant that by late afternoon the shield wall had almost disintegrated.

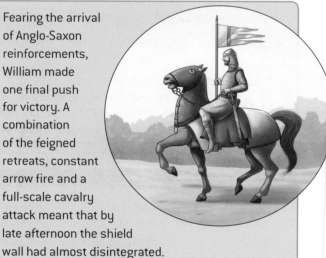

5

As the shield wall fell, the Anglo-Saxons were cut to pieces by the advancing Normans. At some point during this part of the battle, King Harold was killed. With their leader dead and the battle lost, many Anglo-Saxons began to drift away. The day was William's.

Why did William win?

Harold's mistakes	William's tactics	Luck
Harold marched straight to battle against William after fighting at Stamford Bridge, without resting his men or gathering more troops.	William's men believed God was on their side – they were fighting under the Papal Banner.	The weather delayed William's invasion.
Harold had disbanded his army because of the harvest.	The Normans were well organised with clear communication around the battlefield and William could be seen by his men.	Hardrada had invaded at the same time as William, forcing Harold to fight at two ends of the country.
Harold was aware of the feigned retreat tactic, but his men still fell for it.	William had archers and cavalry.	William's army had time to rest before the battle.
Harold was on foot with his men. This showed them that he was willing to fight alongside them, but it also limited his ability to command his army.	William chose the battle site.	

SUMMARY

- William prepared thoroughly for his invasion. This included building a new fleet, raising an army and securing the support of the Pope.

- Harold Godwinson was ready for William's attack but disbanded his army because of the harvest.

- Harald Hardrada invaded in the north. He defeated one Anglo-Saxon army but was defeated himself by Harold Godwinson who had marched 300 km (190 miles) in four days.

- William landed at Pevensey on the south coast and the Anglo-Saxons marched back down the country.

- For a variety of reasons, William defeated Harold at the Battle of Hastings.

 APPLY

WRITE AN ACCOUNT

a Create a flowchart showing the key events of the battle.

b **EXAM QUESTION** Write an account of the Battle of Hastings.

 EXAMINER TIP

Remember to include the reasons for the outcome of the battle in your answer.

HISTORIC ENVIRONMENT

a Create a set of flashcards, one for each of the factors in William's victory shown in the table above. You could add additional factors if you like.

b Can you organise them into long-term (before the battle) factors and short-term (during the battle) factors?

c Organise the cards in order of how important each factor was in William's victory.

d **EXAM QUESTION** 'Mistakes by an opponent were often the most important factor in deciding the outcome of battles in this period.' How far does your study of the Battle of Hastings show this? Explain your answer. You should refer to the Battle of Hastings and your contextual knowledge.

 EXAMINER TIP

Remember for a 'historic environment' question about a battle site you need to consider the following:

- Who fought?
- Where was it fought?
- What happened in the battle?
- Who won and why?

REVIEW

For more guidance on how to answer the 'historic environment' question, turn to page 9.

RECAP

King William's leadership and government

William's next steps

Despite victory at Hastings, William was far from secure in his position. In the following months, he took steps to strengthen his grip on England.

- He moved east to Kent to secure the ports in order to stop Anglo-Saxon trade and allow supplies to be brought in from Normandy.
- He strengthened his fortifications, building motte and bailey castles as he moved towards London.
- He secured control of Canterbury, the centre of the English Catholic Church.
- He burnt Southwark in retaliation for resistance in London.
- He secured Winchester, the base of the English treasury, where the royal income was collected and gold, silver and other valuables were held.
- At a meeting in Berkhamsted he insisted on an oath of loyalty from Edgar the Aetheling (an alternative king supported by the Witan and Stigand, the Archbishop of Canterbury), Edwin and Morcar and a number of other leading nobles and bishops.
- He had himself crowned on Christmas Day, 1066. The ceremony took place in Westminster Abbey in London, the church built by Edward the Confessor.
- At the beginning of 1067, he began distributing land among loyal Norman barons to reward their support and bring security and order to his new kingdom.

> **REVIEW** ↻
>
> Look back at the two previous chapters to remind yourself of who Edgar the Aetheling, Edwin and Morcar were.

Stigand

- Stigand, a bishop, had been a major figure in the court of Edward the Confessor.
- He had a reputation for corruption.
- By the time of the Norman invasion, he was Archbishop of Canterbury.
- William refused to be crowned by Stigand and removed him from his position in 1070.

The Bayeux Tapestry

The tapestry (which is actually an embroidery) tells the story of 1066 from a Norman perspective. Completed in the 1070s under the supervision of William's half-brother, Bishop Odo, it is seen by most as a piece of Norman **propaganda**. It depicts Harold Godwinson as an oath breaker and William as a superior general, as well as the rightful heir to the English throne. Artefacts like the Bayeux Tapestry show the way in which William was able to establish his legitimacy as the rightful king without relying entirely on violence.

 **APPLY**

EXPLAIN

a Create a spider diagram showing the ways in which William had established control by the beginning of 1067.

b Now categorise his actions by completing the table below:

Use of violence	No violence

WRITE AN ACCOUNT

a Create a storyboard showing the key events between the Battle of Hastings and the end of 1066.

b EXAM QUESTION Write an account of how William established control over England up to the beginning of 1067.

EXAMINER TIP

For a 'write an account' question you need to include specific detail. Here you could include specific detail about what William did to establish control.

REVIEW

You may want to include information about motte and bailey castles when answering this exam question. Use pages 28–29 to help you.

Castles

The development of castles

▲ *A modern interpretation of a motte and bailey castle, showing peasants living within the bailey*

The first castles built by the Normans were wooden structures known as motte and bailey castles. They could be built in a matter of weeks, often using the natural features of the landscape. The first motte and bailey was built at Pevensey in the days after William landed there, in September 1066. In the months following the Battle of Hastings, castles were built all over England. By 1070, wood had been replaced by stone for most new castles. By 1086, around 48 large castles and many other smaller ones had been built in England.

The purpose of castles

Castles were built for several reasons:

- To act as a centre of *administration* for an area.
- To *protect* Norman settlers, particularly the new lords.
- To *intimidate* the local population and show power. Building castles involved moving large amounts of earth and stone and clearing forests, which demonstrated the strength and power of the Norman invaders.
- To establish *control* of an area – this was particularly important in places like the north of England and the Welsh border.
- A clear way of demonstrating the social structure of Norman England – the Norman rulers lived in castles on the top of hills and their Anglo-Saxon subjects lived at the bottom. A castle was a highly visible *symbol* that all could understand.

Outer bailey: The area within the outer wall. This included houses and other buildings that needed to be kept safe. At Pevensey, the Normans extended the existing Roman ruins.

Outer bailey wall: Very high walls with plenty of lookout posts. The slightly raised ground leading up to the wall made it difficult to attack.

Moat: Most moats, including Pevensey's, were dry ditches, although some contained water. At Pevensey, the Normans used the old Roman ditch.

Inner bailey: The area within the inner wall that protects the keep. The last line of defence.

Motte: A mound of earth with a keep on top. At some castles this was very steep. It was less clear at Pevensey because the bailey is naturally raised above the surrounding area.

Gateways and gatehouses: Entrances into the outer and inner baileys. Soldiers were positioned at the gateways to offer protection at the castle's most vulnerable points. Some castles had drawbridges.

REVISION SKILLS

Mnemonics can be a useful way to remember important information. For example, when learning the purpose of castles, remember **APICS**:

Administration

Protection

Intimidation

Control

Symbolism

Where were castles built?

- In areas of strategic importance – e.g. on old Roman roads or river crossings.
- On high ground – to see attackers coming.
- Near existing towns.
- Near a water supply and other resources – e.g. wood.
- Near natural defences – e.g. the bend in a river or on the coast.

Pevensey Castle

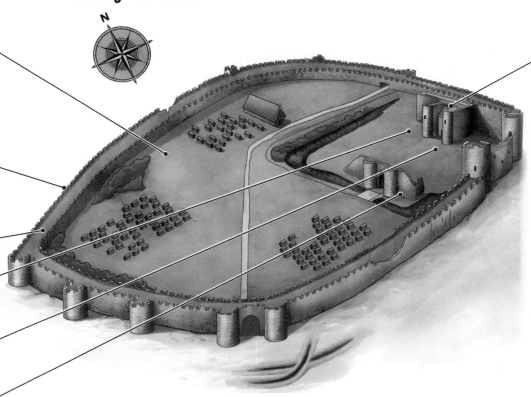

Keep: Initially built of wood, but later stone, and built on top of the motte. High, straight walls made it difficult to climb and soldiers were constantly positioned to spot an attack early and defend the castle. A steep, narrow staircase and crenellations (battlements) helped to make it the most secure part of the castle.

▲ An artist's impression of what Pevensey Castle would have looked like in Norman times; Pevensey's coastal location allowed for easier communication with Normandy

⚙ APPLY

HISTORIC ENVIRONMENT

a Make a list of the key features of a castle.

b Now make a list of the key reasons for building a castle. Match each feature from **a** to one of these reasons (or 'purposes').

c (EXAM QUESTION) 'The main purpose of Norman castles was to intimidate the local population.' How far does a study of Pevensey Castle reflect this statement? Explain your answer. You should refer to Pevensey Castle and your contextual knowledge.

EXPLAIN

(EXAM QUESTION) Explain the importance of castles in Norman England.

EXAMINER TIP Remember to include plenty of your own knowledge of castles and England after the Battle of Hastings.

REVISION SKILLS You could create your own mnemonic to help remember the reasons why castles were built.

EXAMINER TIP For this question you will need to include your contextual knowledge of England under William I. Why did he feel the need to build castles?

Revolts against the Normans

King William now had two realms to control: England and Normandy. In the early years of his reign revolts against Norman rule broke out in different parts of England.

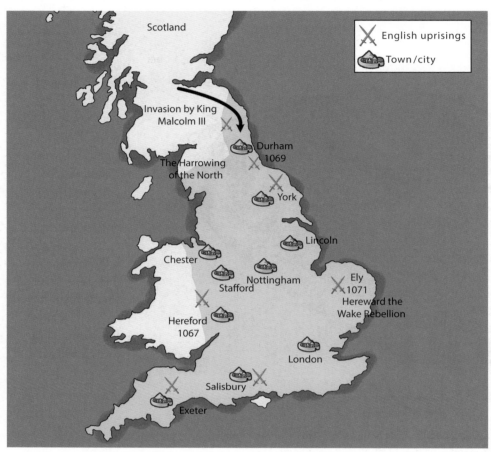

▲ *The location of the English uprisings against Norman rule*

Edwin and Morcar

Brothers Edwin and Morcar had been powerful figures under King Harold. As well as being Harold's brothers-in-law, they had led the Anglo-Saxon army into battle against Harald Hardrada at Fulford Gate. They led a rebellion in London immediately after the Battle of Hastings but it was soon put down by the Normans. They were forced to swear an oath of loyalty to William in Berkhamsted before his coronation. He allowed them to keep all their lands and titles.

The rebellion of the Welsh border

The Welsh borders had proved a challenging place to control for Anglo-Saxon and Viking kings, and William was no different. Problems arose in 1067 when a Herefordshire thegn, Edric the Wild, started a revolt with a large number of Anglo-Saxon followers and the support of the Welsh princes. The rebellion failed to take hold but when he launched a second attack in 1069 he was more successful, reaching Cheshire and Staffordshire. The rebels reached the gates of Shrewsbury Castle but William personally led a group of soldiers up the country to defeat them.

Timeline

▼ **1066**

- Rebellion by Edwin and Morcar in London

▼ **1067**

- Unrest along the Welsh border and in Hertfordshire

▼ **1068**

- Rebellions in the south-west
- Siege of Exeter by William
- Harold Godwinson's sons land in Somerset

▼ **1069**

- Second rebellion by the Welsh princes.

▼ **1075**

- Revolt of the Norman earls

The revolt of Eustace

Edward the Confessor's brother-in-law, Eustace, Count of Boulogne, attacked Dover Castle, which had been left in the care of Bishop Odo while William was back in Normandy. Eustace was easily defeated by the knights of the castle and later made peace with William.

The south-west and Exeter

The city of Exeter rebelled against William in 1068. William dealt with the uprising by besieging the city for 18 days. When Exeter eventually surrendered, the king built a castle there and left his half-brother, Robert of Mortain, in command. On his return journey to London, William was forced to suppress rebellions in Bristol and Gloucester. Around the same time, three of Harold Godwinson's sons landed in Somerset but were unsuccessful in their attempt to retake the throne.

The revolt of the Norman earls

In 1075, William faced an unexpected rebellion from his own Norman earls. It was led by Ralph de Gael and Roger de Breteuil and supported by a number of key figures including an English earl named Waltheof. The rebellion was also encouraged by the king of France who was keen to distract William from Normandy in order to increase his own influence there. The rebellion was a serious threat to William, although he chose to leave it to his allies to deal with. Bishops Odo and Lanfranc put down the rebellion with brutal force. Waltheof was beheaded while other rebels were blinded and killed. Roger was imprisoned but spared more serious punishment, perhaps because of the king's friendship with his father.

 **APPLY**

EXPLAIN

a Create a 50-word summary of the revolt of the Norman earls. Now try 20 words, and finally 10.

b What makes this revolt different to the other revolts?

c **EXAM QUESTION** Explain the importance of the revolt of the Norman earls in 1075.

 EXAMINER TIP

Remember, when considering the importance of an event, you need to put it in a wider context. What else was happening in England at the time? Who was powerful? Were there other rebellions?

WRITE AN ACCOUNT

a Create a revision poster that covers the key aspects of each of the revolts against William.

b **EXAM QUESTION** Write an account of the rebellions faced by William between 1066 and 1075.

 EXAMINER TIP

Remember to make links between the rebellions; don't just look at them as unrelated events.

REVIEW

The next four pages deal with the Harrying of the North and the rebellion of Hereward the Wake. You might want to revisit this question once you have read these pages.

 **RECAP**

The Harrying of the North

The causes

Tensions in the north of England had existed since William's invasion but they reached boiling point in 1068/69.

- Edwin, Morcar and Edgar the Aetheling fled north in 1068. Edgar once again made a claim on William's throne.
- King Malcolm of Scotland, who had recently married Edgar's sister, gave his support to the claim. Edgar was becoming a powerful rival to William.
- In January 1069, a Norman earl, Robert of Commines, was murdered by a group of English rebels and the Bishop of Durham's house was set on fire.
- Edgar attacked the city of York.
- In the summer, 240 Danish Viking ships invaded the north of England and joined Edgar's army.
- This army took control of York Castle and defeated the Norman army stationed in the city.

REVIEW ⟳

Look back at pages 14, 26 and 30 to remind yourself who Edgar, Edwin and Morcar were.

What happened next?

William's response was brutal.

- He paid the Vikings to abandon the English army and return to Denmark. The leaders of the English army scattered.
- Determined to teach the people of the north a lesson, William laid waste to huge areas of land around York. He ordered the slaughter of all livestock, the burning of all crops and the salting of the land so that nothing else could grow.
- It is William's response that is known as the 'Harrying of the North' rather than the rebellion that led to it.

The consequences

- The immediate consequences were farmers' loss of income and starvation of peasants across the region.
- In the Domesday Book, written in 1086, 80 per cent of Yorkshire was recorded as 'waste', meaning that it was unpopulated and not used for farming. This may have been the direct result of William's actions.
- William's aim had been to remove the threat of rebellion in the north once and for all and it is certainly true that he faced little trouble from Yorkshire again during his reign. The Harrying did not, however, mark the end of rebellions against William elsewhere in the country.

REVIEW

Look back at pages 30–31 and read the next two pages for more information about other rebellions against the Normans. Make sure you are clear about which ones took place before the Harrying of the North and which ones came after it.

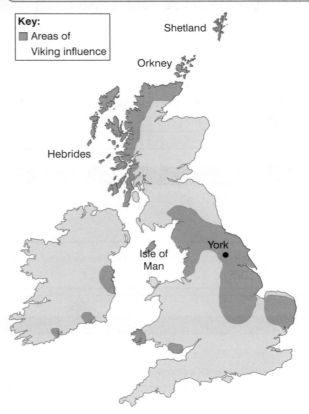

▲ *This map shows the areas of Viking influence, where people tended to be more rebellious and caused problems for William*

 **APPLY**

INTERPRETATION ANALYSIS

Read **Interpretation A**.

▼ **INTERPRETATION A** *Adapted from William the Conqueror's deathbed confession, recorded in a church history book called* The Ecclesiastical History *by Orderic Vitalis (1123–1141):*

> William fell on the English of the northern shires like a ravening lion. He commanded their houses and corn, with all their possessions, to be burnt without distinction, and large herds of cattle and beasts of burden to be butchered wherever they were found. And by doing so alas he became the barbarous murderer of many thousands, both young and old, of that fine race of people.

a In no more than 15 words, describe what the interpretation says about the Harrying of the North.

_____

_____

_____

b Does the interpretation reflect what you know about the events of the Harrying of the North?

_____

_____

_____

_____

c

> **EXAM QUESTION** How convincing is **Interpretation A** about William's actions in the Harrying of the North? Explain your answer based on your contextual knowledge and what it says in **Interpretation A**.

 EXAMINER TIP

You cannot answer an interpretation question until you are clear about what the interpretation says. Make sure you read it carefully and can summarise its meaning in your head. Even if you are not clear on the meaning of some words, you can still understand the interpretation as a whole.

WRITE AN ACCOUNT

a Create a storyboard that tells the story of the Harrying of the North. Make sure you include the causes, events and consequences.

b Why do you think William responded to events in the north in the way that he did?

c

> **EXAM QUESTION** Write an account of how events in the north of England led to the Harrying of the North.

 EXAMINER TIP

Select two events and suggest why they might have provoked such a violent response from William.

REVISION SKILLS

Having someone test you on your notes and revision is an excellent way of seeing how much you remember, understand, and still have to learn. Brief oral test sessions of about 10 minutes are best.

Hereward the Wake

The rebellion of Hereward the Wake in the early 1070s is one of the best-known rebellions of the Norman period.

What happened?

- Hereward's father was believed to be Leofric, Earl of Mercia.
- He was angry that William and the Normans had confiscated land from his father and killed his brother.
- With the support of King Swegn of Denmark and Morcar (Edwin had been killed), Hereward began a campaign of **guerrilla**-style attacks on Norman settlers in the marshes and fenlands of East Anglia. His men fought in small groups and hid to take the enemy by surprise.
- Hereward's supporters were able to use their knowledge of the land to avoid capture and frustrate William's attempts to end the rebellion in the way he had others.
- Their most famous attack was the looting and burning of Peterborough Abbey in 1070.
- The rebels were based at the abbey on the Isle of Ely, which was well defended and surrounded by marshland.

Having paid King Swegn to leave England, William turned his attention to Morcar and Hereward. Unable to attack directly, he besieged the Isle of Ely and made several attempts to cross the marshland.

ATTEMPT 1:

William ordered the building of a 3km (2 miles) wooden causeway to cross the marshland. The structure was strong and impressive.

FAILED:

The causeway was not strong enough for the sheer number of Norman soldiers who tried to cross it and it collapsed.

ATTEMPT 2:

William built a siege tower and, according to some accounts, found a local witch to stand at the top of the tower and shout abuse and curses at the rebels.

FAILED:

Hereward set fire to the area and the tower burnt down.

ATTEMPT 3:

William convinced the monks of Ely Abbey to reveal a secret route to Hereward's base.

SUCCEEDED:

William reached the abbey and arrested most of the rebels, including Morcar. Hereward, however, escaped.

SUMMARY

- After his victory at Hastings, William needed to establish control quickly.

- His early actions included forcing rivals to swear loyalty and taking control of key parts of the country. He also gave land to loyal Normans.

- William built castles across the country. Initially these were motte and bailey castles, but they developed and changed over time.

- There were a number of rebellions against William's rule, most of which were dealt with quickly.

- In response to unrest, William devastated the area around York in what became known as the 'Harrying of the North'.

- One famous challenge William faced was the rebellion of Hereward the Wake in East Anglia.

 **APPLY**

WRITE AN ACCOUNT

a   Create a flowchart to show the key events shown on these pages.

b   Look back at pages 30–31. How does the rebellion of Hereward the Wake differ from other rebellions that William faced?

c   EXAM QUESTION Write an account of the rebellion of Hereward the Wake.

 EXAMINER TIP

Make sure you tell the full story of the rebellion, not just the events at Ely.

REVISION SKILLS

Remember that the exam rewards you for accurate spelling, punctuation and grammar (SPaG) — make sure you get into good habits as you revise!

EXPLAIN

a   Make a list of any common features of Hereward's rebellion and the others you have studied. For example, the involvement of Morcar.

b   Outline the ways in which Anglo-Saxon earls had become involved in rebellions against William.

c   EXAM QUESTION Explain what was important about the roles of Anglo-Saxon nobles in rebellions against William?

 EXAMINER TIP

This question is asking you about all rebellions that involved Anglo-Saxon earls, so make sure you include a range of specific examples.

REVISION SKILLS

Use sketches, doodles, and pictures to help make facts memorable. You do not have to be a good artist to do this!

Feudalism and government

CHAPTER 4

RECAP

Feudalism

Anglo-Saxon and Norman government

Although the Normans introduced the feudal system to England, there is debate about how far the feudal system was new or a development of an existing system. Before the Norman invasion, England was divided into earldoms, governed by earls who could become incredibly powerful (Godwin of Wessex is a good example). The king could make anyone an earl and give them a piece of land. In return he expected their loyalty (this was known as **patronage**). However, he was also free to take away land and could call upon his earls to provide an army in times of war.

Landholding and lordship under William

In order to recruit Normans and mercenaries to fight for him at Hastings, William promised them land once England had been taken.

- At first, William allowed most Anglo-Saxons to keep their earldoms. However, he split the large areas that were without an earl (generally because they had been killed at Hastings – Wessex, whose earl had been King Harold, was an example of this) into smaller areas and appointed Normans to govern them. These men were known as **barons** or **tenants-in-chief**.

- Gradually he replaced other English earls with Normans and gave them their lands to create a Norman aristocracy. As Anglo-Saxon earls died or rebelled against William they were replaced with Normans. William gave the new Norman aristocracy the lands of the Anglo-Saxon earls.

- A small number of the barons became particularly powerful. These included William's two half-brothers, Robert of Mortmain and Bishop Odo, and a distant cousin, William Fitzosbern.

- By 1076, only two earldoms were still held by Anglo-Saxons.

The feudal system

This diagram shows the structure of English society under the Normans.

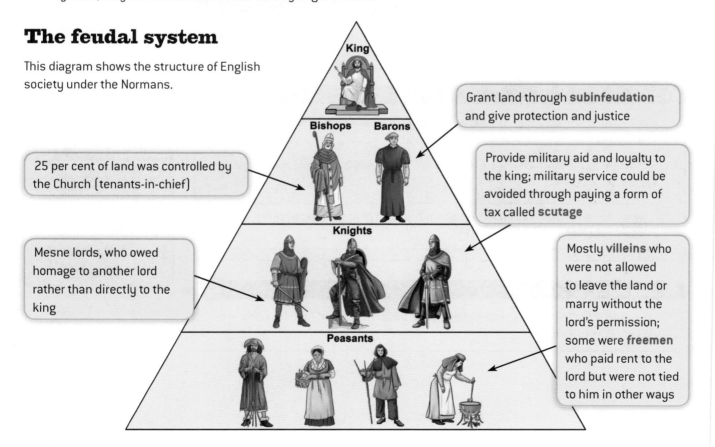

King

Grant land through **subinfeudation** and give protection and justice

Bishops   Barons

25 per cent of land was controlled by the Church (tenants-in-chief)

Provide military aid and loyalty to the king; military service could be avoided through paying a form of tax called **scutage**

Knights

Mesne lords, who owed homage to another lord rather than directly to the king

Mostly **villeins** who were not allowed to leave the land or marry without the lord's permission; some were **freemen** who paid rent to the lord but were not tied to him in other ways

Peasants

 **APPLY**

INTERPRETATION ANALYSIS

Read the interpretation below:

▼ **INTERPRETATION A** *Adapted from a history textbook by Andrew Holland and Nicholas Fellows, published in 2015:*

> Despite elements of continuity, the changes were great, and kings and barons certainly had much more power over their men than had been the situation before the conquest... The king was able to exploit his feudal rights and also created a new feudal aristocracy, but this was within the Anglo-Saxon state.

a Does the interpretation suggest that the Norman feudal system was a change from, or a development of, the Anglo-Saxon system?

_____

_____

b Do you agree with the interpretation? Why?

_____

_____

_____

_____

c **EXAM QUESTION** How convincing is **Interpretation A** about the feudal system introduced by William I? Explain your answer based on your contextual knowledge and what it says in **Interpretation A**.

 EXAMINER TIP

Remember you need to include details from the interpretation as well as specific contextual knowledge to support your answer.

EXPLAIN

a Make a list of the ways in which the feudal system benefited William.

_____

_____

_____

_____

b **EXAM QUESTION** Explain the importance of the feudal system in Norman England.

EXAMINER TIP

You need to explain what the feudal system was and how it worked before going on to explain what role it played in Norman society.

The Domesday Book

What was the Domesday Book?

The Domesday Survey (which later became the Domesday Book) was the biggest gathering of information in English history. It was carried out in 1086, and in its written form, during the reign of William II, it became an invaluable source of evidence for historians. There are a number of theories as to why William I ordered the Domesday Survey. Some of the main reasons considered are:

- to help collect taxes accurately and so ensure that William got as much money as possible.
- to make sure feudal lords were not hiding wealth that could be used to threaten his position.
- to record and settle arguments over land that existed after the invasion.
- to make it clear that all land was held by permission of the king.

The survey investigated:

- who lived where and who owned what land and property
- the overall value of each man's property, including animals and ploughs
- what taxes were owed from the time of Edward the Confessor
- who held wealth (and therefore power) in different parts of the country.

The survey showed that:

- William and his family owned about 20 per cent of the land
- the Church held around 25 per cent
- around 10 members of the Norman aristocracy held 25 per cent between them
- 170 others held the remaining 30 per cent.

Land ownership under William

This meant that just 250 people held all of the land in England. This was similar to the situation under Edward the Confessor, except that the land was now mostly controlled by Normans.

Technically, all land belonged to the king and he was free to distribute it as he saw fit.

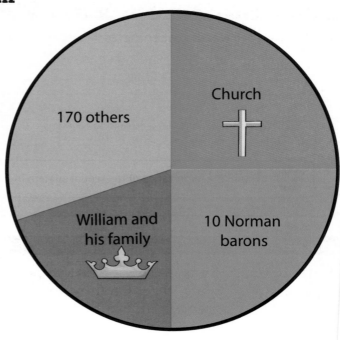

▲ *Land ownership under William*

It tells us who owned the land (see the pie chart on the previous page).

The extent to which William had replaced Anglo-Saxon earls and landlords with Norman ones.

There were 2000 knights in England.

What does Domesday tell us about life in Norman England?

How landholding had changed between the rule of King Edward and the rule of King William (Anglo-Saxon to Norman).

There were around 10,000 Norman settlers in total.

The total population of England was between 1.5 and 2 million people.

 APPLY

EXPLAIN

a Create a mind-map on the Domesday Survey. Make sure you include the following:

- what it was
- why it was carried out
- what it investigated
- what it revealed.

b Make a list of the ways in which the Domesday Survey is useful for understanding Norman England.

c **EXAM QUESTION** Explain the importance of the Domesday Survey in Norman England.

INTERPRETATION ANALYSIS

Read the interpretation below:

▼ **INTERPRETATION A** *From an article in the* Spectator *magazine written by Ed West, published in October 2016:*

> The conquest was certainly disastrous for the native aristocracy. Those who survived Hastings were thrown off their land, and by the time of the Conqueror's death just 5 per cent of England was owned by the natives, with between a third and half of the country shared out between 170 Norman barons, and the rest going to the king and the Church; there were just two English major landowners left.

a What opinion does the interpretation have of William I's changes?

b Does the interpretation reflect your knowledge of what happened in England under the Normans?

c **EXAM QUESTION** How convincing is **Interpretation A** about the impact of the Norman Conquest on England? Explain your answer based on your contextual knowledge and what it says in **Interpretation A**.

Justice and the legal system

Although the Normans maintained much of the Anglo-Saxon system of law and order, they did make a number of changes to what had existed before 1066.

Anglo-Saxon	Norman
Shire courts Shire courts met twice a year when the **sheriff** would hear cases involving land disputes, crime, taxes and rebellions.	• Castles were built in shire towns (the main town of an area) and all administration was based in them. This included the sheriff and court. • Shire courts declined in importance due to **honorial courts** where tenants could appeal directly to their lord. • Royal household officials were sent to courts to oversee proceedings and, in some cases, juries were introduced.
Hundred courts Shires were divided into small areas known as **hundreds**. Hundred courts dealt with local land issues.	The hundred courts met more frequently than shire courts and were run by the sheriff's deputy.
Inheritance It was common to divide up landholdings among the family when someone died.	The stability of the feudal system relied on earldoms not being split. The Normans established the idea of **primogeniture** – where the eldest son inherits everything.
The oath system Anglo-Saxons often made a promise not to be involved in crime, known as the 'common oath'. If they did commit a crime, their whole family could be punished. Punishment could include exile.	The Normans introduced **murdrum fines**. If any Norman was murdered, all Anglo-Saxons in the area would be heavily fined. The aim was to protect the many new Norman earls now in power over the Anglo-Saxon populace, as they were vulnerable to attack.
Punishments Punishments tended to be brutal, with execution and mutilation relatively common. Another form of punishment was based on the 'ordeal system'. This was based on the principle of '*Judicium Dei*' (the Judgement of God). The accused was put through a painful ordeal, such as 'ordeal by fire' or 'ordeal by water', to test their guilt. It was believed that God would save the innocent.	Most Anglo-Saxon punishments were maintained, with the addition of 'ordeal by combat'. This involved the accuser and accused fighting, usually to the death. The winner would be presumed to have been telling the truth about the crime.

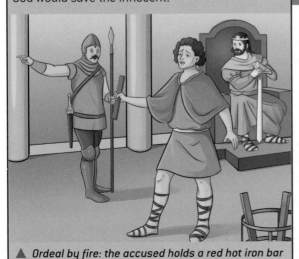
▲ *Ordeal by fire: the accused holds a red hot iron bar*

Anglo-Saxon		Norman
The language of law Law had been recorded in English.	→	Laws were recorded in Latin and it became the official language of the government and the Church.
Forest laws Prior to the Norman invasion, people had been allowed to hunt animals in the forests to supplement their diets.	→	William was a keen hunter and unwilling to allow ordinary people to hunt on his lands. He introduced forest laws that banned the activity. Punishments for breaking these laws included fines, mutilations (for example, being blinded) and execution.

 APPLY

EXPLAIN

a Complete the table to show change and continuity between the Anglo-Saxon and the Norman approaches to law and order.

Change	Continuity

 EXAMINER TIPP

For this question, you need to give a detailed explanation of exactly what the Normans changed from what had gone before.

b **EXAM QUESTION** Explain what was important about the changes the Normans made to law and order in England.

WRITE AN ACCOUNT

 EXAM QUESTION Write an account of the ways in which the system of law changed under William I.

 EXAMINER TIP

Make sure you give a clear explanation about the consequences of the changes, as well as describing what changed.

REVIEW

After reading a couple of pages of a textbook, revision guide or your notes, ask yourself 'What are the six most important things I need to remember?' Write those down on a piece of paper. Don't worry about the things you have forgotten, you will remember those next time!

REVISION SKILLS

Reducing information to a shorter, more concise form is a valuable exercise.

The death of William II

Background

William I had three sons: Robert, William and Henry. Robert had a poor relationship with both his father and his younger brother William. In the hope of avoiding conflict after his death, and because he did not believe Robert had the ability to govern the whole country, William declared that the inheritance would be split: Robert (known as Robert Curthose) would have Normandy, William would rule England and Henry would receive the substantial sum of £5000. This went against the Norman tradition of primogeniture and Robert was unhappy with it. He believed that as the eldest son he should rule both Normandy and England. After a final, major argument with his father, Robert fled over the Channel to his uncle in Flanders. Once William II (also known as William Rufus) was crowned, Robert rebelled against the new king and major disagreements continued.

How did William II die?

In 1100, William II travelled to the New Forest to go hunting. Shortly after his arrival he told his companions that he had had a dream in which he had been killed. While out hunting that day, William Rufus was shot and killed with an arrow. It is likely that a nobleman named William Tirel fired the arrow as he fled immediately after the incident happened. However, it has never been firmly established if it was an accident or if someone had told him to do it. Regardless, William's younger brother Henry became king and the Tirel family grew in wealth in the early years of his reign.

Who was to blame? The main suspects

Suspect: Robert Curthose

Motives: He believed that he was the rightful King of England and that he had had his inheritance taken from him. He led a rebellion against William II in 1088 and attempted an invasion of England in early 1100.

Suspect: Henry (later Henry I)

Motives: The youngest of William I's sons. With Rufus dead and Robert in exile, he became king in 1100.

Suspect: Archbishop Anselm

Motives: William II argued with Anselm, the Archbishop of Canterbury, who felt William was too involved in Church affairs. Anselm fled England for Rome in 1097 and William seized all of his land.

Suspect: Members of the nobility

Motives: With his high taxes and harsh rule, William II was unpopular with many of the people of England, both rich and poor. His temper also made him unpredictable. It has been suggested that some members of the nobility felt England would prosper under a different king.

SUMMARY

- The Normans introduced changes to the structure of society in what became known as the feudal system.

- The Domesday Survey was carried out in 1086 to establish who owned what land and owed tax to the king.

- The Normans largely continued the Anglo-Saxon system of law and order but did make a number of changes.

- William Rufus succeeded William I as King of England despite being his second son. This caused conflict with Robert, his elder brother.

- William Rufus was killed in mysterious circumstances in 1100 and was succeeded by his younger brother Henry.

 APPLY

EXPLAIN

a Create a timeline of the key events leading to William II's death. Start with William I's decision to split the inheritance between his sons.

b Add or highlight any key events on your timeline that could be seen as evidence against one of the suspects.

c Explain what was important about the murder of William Rufus.

EXAMINER TIP

Remember to include background information and to consider the possible suspects. Don't just tell the story of the murder.

INTERPRETATION ANALYSIS

Read the interpretation below:

▼ **INTERPRETATION A** *Adapted from* A History of England *by Roger of Wendover, a monk, written sometime before 1236*:

> In 1094 William demanded the sum of one thousand pounds from Anselm without delay, asserting that he had the right to demand it... But Anselm considered he could not fill the King's coffers without damaging his own conscience. He then asked the King's permission to go to Rome... William was violently incensed and asserted that no archbishop of his dominions should pay respect to the court of the Pope in Rome. Anselm was brought before the King and accused of high treason.

a Rewrite the interpretation in your own words.

b Does the source provide evidence that Anselm should be considered a suspect in William's murder? What does it tell you about their relationship?

Copy and complete the table below:

Suspect	Not a suspect

c How convincing is **Interpretation A** about the difficult relationship between Anselm and William II? Explain your answer based on your contextual knowledge and what it says in **Interpretation A**.

EXAMINER TIP

Remember to use your own knowledge about William and Anselm's disagreements about Church affairs.

CHAPTER 5

Economic and social changes

 **RECAP**

Village life in Norman England

For most peasants, life after the Norman invasion was exactly the same as before – just with a new lord.

- Peasants lived in cottages, grew crops on strips of land and grazed animals on the common land.
- The strips were not separated by hedges – this was known as the open field system.
- The lord kept up to 35 per cent of the land. The peasants had the rest, although they had to pay rent to the lord.
- Metal ploughs were pulled by oxen.
- The main crops were wheat, barley, oats and rye.
- Houses were built along roads and were clustered together.
- There was a clear division between land for houses, farmland, pasture for animals and woodland.
- The church bells were rung to signal the beginning and end of the working day.
- They got up half an hour before sunrise and worked until sunset.
- Lunch would usually just be rye bread; in the evening they would usually eat a vegetable-based meal. They would usually drink weak homemade beer or cider.
- Church services were held on Sundays, and on feast days and holy days ('holidays').
- Peasants would work every day except Sundays and holy days. Days off would include leisure activities like cock fighting.
- All peasants had to pay a 10 per cent tax (tithe) to the Church.
- The local church also acted as a store, a prison and a fortress in times of danger.

Peasants' homes

Houses were usually cold, damp and dark. The walls were made of wattle and daub. They usually had small windows to keep in warmth and stop break-ins. Most families had a single room and animals would often be brought into the house. The thatched roofs were vulnerable to fire.

The manor

The manor was a specific area within the village.
- It was the area owned directly by the lord and was known as his **demesne**.
- It included the manor house, where the lord lived, as well as the homes of the peasants known as freemen.
- Thegns, knights and barons often owned land of around 485–730 hectares (1200–1800 acres) in size. They would also have owned houses, barns, woods and lakes in and around the manor.
- The manor house itself was made of stone and was much warmer and more secure than the peasants' houses.

Roles and responsibilities

In addition to the lord and the ordinary peasants there were also several other important roles:

Reeve: chosen by the lord or by peasant vote. Although more powerful under the Anglo-Saxons, after 1066 their job was to manage the day-to-day running of the manor and ensure the peasants were all working.

Bailiff: responsible for collecting taxes for the king and ensuring crops were gathered and debts repaid.

Priest: responsible for marriages and wills, as well as running the local church and conducting services.

Miller: produced grain to make bread for the whole village.

A peasant's year

Spring: peasants sow seeds in the fields

Summer: when the crops are ready, peasants harvest them

Autumn: peasants used oxen to plough the fields before planting next year's crop

Winter: people lived off the food harvested earlier in the year

⚙ APPLY

WRITE AN ACCOUNT

a Make a simple copy of the village map shown on the opposite page. Now annotate it with information about the lives of the people that lived in the village under the Normans.

b Using two colours, highlight examples of continuity from Anglo-Saxons times and examples of things that had changed under the Normans.

c **EXAM QUESTION** Write an account of the ways in which the lives of Anglo-Saxon villagers stayed the same under the Normans.

EXAMINER TIP 🎯

In order to consider whether life did stay the same, you will need to show a good knowledge of life before and after the Norman invasion.

REVIEW 🔄

You may wish to look at pages 48–49 before you answer this question.

EXPLAIN

a Make a list of the different roles within a Norman village and describe briefly what each role did. Include the ones from the table above and others from the rest of this section.

b Imagine removing one of these roles. What would happen to the village and its people?

 **RECAP**

Key features of a Norman town

- Houses were built closely together and living conditions were cramped.
- Castles were at the centre of many larger towns and became centres of trade.
- Other towns had cathedrals at their centre (some, like Lincoln, had both).
- **Burgesses** were important figures in towns. They had the right to buy and sell property but owed tax and services to the local lord. In some areas they handled legal issues for the shire or the hundred.

REVIEW

Revisit pages 40–41 to remind yourself about shires and hundreds in Norman England.

The growth of towns

- After the invasion, existing towns grew in importance as administrative or religious centres.
- London and Norwich became increasingly important as administrative centres. Winchester's importance declined, but a new cathedral made it religiously significant.
- Norman nobles encouraged towns to grow as a way of developing foreign trade, particularly in the south. Towns were able to specialise in a particular product or material.
- Between 1066 and 1100, 21 new towns developed.
- Evidence of this growth can be found in the Domesday Survey.

Metalwork

Towns like Gloucester became centres of iron and lead production, important for house building and making weapons. These towns tended to be located near woodland so that they were able to use the wood in their furnaces.

The role of trade in the growth of towns

Salt

Towns like Droitwich grew as a result of the production and sale of salt, used in cooking and food preservation.

Wool

Although produced in the countryside, wool was brought to towns like Lincoln and York to be sold at the markets. It was exported to the rest of Europe so many coastal towns became centres of international trade.

Markets and fairs

To hold a market or a fair, a town needed a special permission (franchise) that was given in the form of a **grant** by the king. William gave out around 2800 grants. Markets were places for traders to buy and sell products and, although fairs were officially religious celebrations, they were also often places of commerce.

Guilds

Weavers, goldsmiths, bakers, butchers and others began to form specialist associations, or **guilds,** in each town. The guilds often had significant power.

APPLY

EXPLAIN

a Make a list of the ways in which trade led to the growth and development of towns in the Norman period.

_____

_____

_____

b **EXAM QUESTION** Explain what was important about trade in the development of Norman towns.

WRITE AN ACCOUNT

a Copy and complete the spider diagram to show the development of towns under the Normans.

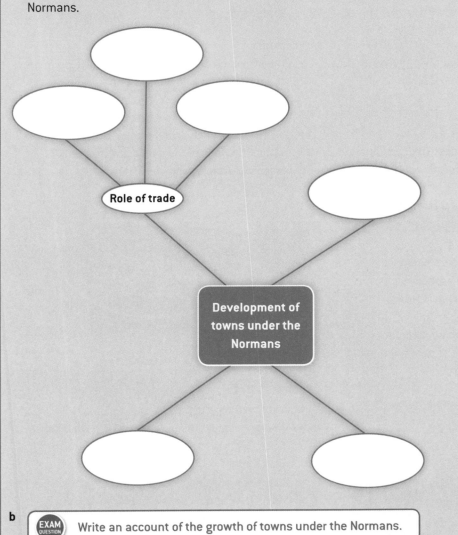

b **EXAM QUESTION** Write an account of the growth of towns under the Normans.

 **RECAP**

Did the Norman Conquest change everyday life?

REVIEW

Look back through pages 36–47 to remind yourself what elements of life changed and what stayed the same under William I.

Land

Norman aristocracy:
- Initially William tried to keep Anglo-Saxon landowners in place, but many took part in rebellions and he replaced them with Normans whom he could trust.
- Before the invasion, a few earls controlled most of the land. William split these earldoms into much smaller areas. This made them less powerful.
- A new group, known as knights, were also able to hold land. Some historians argue that knights were in fact just the Norman version of the Anglo-Saxon thegns.

Peasants:
- Life for peasants changed very little. They just had a new lord to work for.

New laws

Norman aristocracy:
- William kept most of the Anglo-Saxon financial system (even introducing some aspects, like the exchequer and the minting system, to Normandy).
- Trial by jury was introduced, although only the Norman aristocracy had the right to demand this.

Peasants:
- New forest laws meant that peasants could no longer hunt to supplement their diets.
- Murdrum fines meant that the whole area would pay for any attack on a Norman.

Castles

Norman aristocracy:
- Castles were built to establish status and protect the new lords from the local Anglo-Saxon population.
- Over time, castles became centres of trade and commerce.

Peasants:
- The size of castles, and the speed at which they could be built, would no doubt have intimidated the local population.
- Land was seized and cleared for the castles.
- Many locals, such as the blacksmith, worked within the walls of the bailey and so were protected from attack.

Language

Norman aristocracy:
- The language of the new aristocracy was French. French was also used at court, in law and in government.
- Latin was still used for religious services.
- As time went on, English and Norman French began to merge to create Anglo-Norman.

Peasants:
- Peasants continued to speak English. Over time, some Norman words began to be used in everyday speech.

SUMMARY

- Life in Norman villages remained largely the same as it was before the invasion. Peasants worked the land and the Church played a key role in everyday life.

- There were a number of key positions within the village. These included the reeve, the bailiff, the priest, the miller and the lord of the manor.

- The peasants' year was highly structured, and they had little time off.

- The number and size of towns increased under the Normans. This was largely because of trade and the growth of markets.

- The extent to which life changed under the Normans varied across society. Peasant life remained largely the same but there were big changes for the aristocracy.

REVISION SKILLS

Try turning the information on these pages into flashcards as a way of revising life under the Normans. On one side write the headings from each box, and on the other briefly outline what changed and what remained the same.

APPLY

INTERPRETATION ANALYSIS

Read the interpretation below.

▼ **INTERPRETATION A** *Adapted from an article in the* Southern Daily Echo, *published in October 2016:*

> The arrival of the Normans meant the ancient Anglo-Saxon culture, laws and ways of living that had evolved since the end of the Roman occupation were replaced by a new way of life brought in by the conquerors. But for ordinary residents the changes may not have been as dramatic or sudden as some historians might have us believe. And while it is true that local rulers were replaced, forts and castles built and new laws did away with some old traditions, much of life… would have gone on as it had before.

a What opinion does the interpretation have of changes under William I?

b Does the interpretation reflect your knowledge of what happened in England under the Normans?

c
> **EXAM QUESTION** How convincing is **Interpretation A** about the impact of the Norman Conquest on England? Explain your answer based on your contextual knowledge and what it says in **Interpretation A**.

EXAMINER TIP

Remember to include your knowledge of change, beyond what is described in the interpretation.

EXPLAIN

a Make a list of the changes that occurred in England after the Norman invasion.

b
> **EXAM QUESTION** Explain what was important about the economic and social changes that occurred in the lives of ordinary people under Norman rule.

EXAMINER TIP

Remember to look at all aspects of life covered on these pages.

The Church

 RECAP

The role of the Church under the Normans

The Normans practised a branch of Christianity called Roman Catholicism, like the Anglo-Saxons before them. The vast majority of the population was Catholic at this time, and religion played an important part in everyday life.

Economics
- The Church was a major landowner and peasants were required to work on Church land for free (if they didn't, they believed God would punish them).
- Tithes (a tax of 10 per cent) were collected on everything that a farm produced.

Religion
- The main role of the Church was to teach people to live a good life which meant they would go to heaven.
- As most people could not read, they learned about heaven and hell from sermons and **doom paintings** on church walls.

Education
- It was the only institution that produced books, which were copied out by monks. This meant that the Church controlled which books were published.

Law
- The Church heard court cases for crimes committed on Church land.

How did the Church influence people's lives?

Politics
- Leading clergy were members of the Witan, which advised the king on national matters.

Health
- People did not understand the causes of disease and it was widely seen as a punishment from God.
- People turned to the Church for help when they were sick — priests might suggest they ask God for forgiveness through prayer, suffering pain or giving money to the Church.

Priests
- Priests were central figures in communities. They led services, helped the sick, heard confessions and baptised children. All members of the community went to the priest for advice, from peasants to the lord of the manor.

Pilgrimage
- Pilgrimages were an important part of people's lives. The wealthy journeyed to Jerusalem in the Holy Land, while others visited holy sites such as monasteries and abbeys in England.

Norman religious buildings

- Cathedrals, abbeys and monasteries were built to show devotion to God. They were also built to dominate the landscape, as castles did, and show the English that the Normans were now in charge. They were often constructed on hilltops and some, like Durham, were even fortified to provide additional security to the area.

- A popular architectural style in Europe at this time was **Romanesque**. Named after the Roman style, it had clean lines, rounded arches and vaulted ceilings.

- Cathedrals were built in the shape of a cross to symbolise the crucifixion of Jesus, and some, like Durham, faced east towards Jerusalem. Other common features included quires (where the choir or monks sat) and a symmetrical design.

▲ *Durham Cathedral began as a Norman chapel in 1072, high above the banks of the River Wear. It developed into one of the most impressive Norman cathedrals in the north of England*

- Cathedrals were the political bases of bishops, who could become very powerful. The Bishop of Durham was given significant power in order to control a rebellious area on behalf of the king. In 1075 he became a prince bishop. This gave him power to raise an army, impose taxes and mint coins to raise income.

- Most cathedrals were staffed by monks. The Norman bishop who built Durham Cathedral, William of St Calais, brought in Benedictine monks to run it.

- Pilgrims often journeyed to cathedrals, monasteries and abbeys, and so many included **shrines** to important saints or holy relics. Durham housed the shrine of St Cuthbert, one of the most revered Anglo-Saxon saints.

REVIEW

Find out more about the Benedictines on page 54.

⚙ APPLY

HISTORIC ENVIRONMENT

a Create a spider diagram showing the key features of a Norman cathedral.

b **EXAM QUESTION** 'The main reason for building Norman cathedrals was to show religious devotion.' How far does a study of Durham Cathedral reflect this statement?

EXPLAIN

a Create a set of flashcards about the role of the Church in Norman England. Make one for each of the branches of the spider diagram on the left-hand page.

b Rank the different roles of the Church in order of importance by arranging the cards.

c **EXAM QUESTION** Explain what was important about the Church in Norman England.

EXAMINER TIP

You will need to consider any alternative reasons for building cathedrals, for example, intimidating the local population or ensuring order, and use the specific features and history of Durham Cathedral to help you answer the question.

REVIEW

You may want to use some of the information on the next two pages to add additional points to your answer.

William and the Church

When William invaded England, he did so under the Papal Banner and in the belief that God was on his side. Once he was king, he set about dealing with what he saw as corruption in the English Church. His four major concerns were:

- **Pluralism** – clergy holding multiple jobs (and getting paid for them). For example, a priest might be in charge of a parish in the south-west and another parish in the north-east, but never visit either of them.

- Simony – selling positions or jobs within the Church

- Nepotism – appointing unqualified family members to positions of power

- Marriage – according to Church law, clergy were required to remain **celibate**. In reality, many priests were married and had children.

Reform of the English Church

Area	Reform
Bishops	• By 1080, there was only one Anglo-Saxon bishop left – William had replaced the others with Normans. • Lanfranc, a Norman, was made Archbishop of Canterbury in 1070, replacing Stigand, an Anglo-Saxon. Lanfranc was given the job of achieving William's reforms.
Architecture	• Churches and cathedrals were rebuilt in the Romanesque style, with its simple yet impressive design.
Organisation	• The Church was given a clear structure. Dioceses (districts overseen by bishops) were divided into archdeaconries, which were then divided into deaneries. • New cathedrals were built in important locations such as Coventry, Salisbury and Lincoln.
Legal issues	• In 1076, the Council of Winchester ordered that only Church courts could try clergy. • William reintroduced 'Peter's Pence', a tax of one pence paid to the Pope from every household.
Parish priests	• Most Anglo-Saxon parish priests remained in their jobs and, despite attempts at reform, many remained married.

The relationship between Norman kings and the Church

The Papacy

William I's relationship with the Papacy (the authority of the Pope) deteriorated as his reign went on. This decline continued under William II.

Reward

William I and William II promoted or rewarded their supporters by giving them religious positions. It was only the Pope or the Church that had the power to do this, though, which caused conflict between the king and the Church.

Wealth

Both William I and William II used the Church to increase their own wealth. They collected geld (a tax) from religious houses (communities of priests, monks and nuns). There is also evidence that the Normans stole gold and silver ornaments from English churches and sent them to churches in Normandy.

Penance

In 1070 Pope Alexander ordered William I to pay penance for the violence of his invasion. The king ordered the building of Battle Abbey on the site of the Battle of Hastings.

Anselm

When Lanfranc died in 1089, William II did not appoint a new Archbishop of Canterbury. Instead, he used it as an opportunity to take from the Church. He eventually appointed Anselm in 1093. The relationship between the two was difficult, as it was clear that Anselm supported Pope Gregory's attempts to increase the independence of the clergy.

The Investiture Controversy

In 1078, the Pope tried to help the Church stay independent by banning kings from appointing bishops and abbots. This caused huge disagreements between the Pope and the kings of Europe over who could appoint senior members of the Church. The Investiture Controversy finally ended in 1122.

SUMMARY

- The Church was a hugely powerful organisation which influenced almost every aspect of people's lives.

- The Normans constructed a large number of cathedrals and abbeys. These showed their devotion to God but were also a demonstration of power.

- After his invasion, William set about reforming the English Church and dealing with corruption.

- William I and William II's relationship with the Papacy deteriorated over time.

REVISION SKILLS

An important skill when revising is reducing lots of information into a clear, more concise form – this is sometimes known as 'chunking'. Go through the information on this page and try to reduce it to no more than an A5 sheet.

⚙ APPLY

WRITE AN ACCOUNT

a Create a rough timeline of the relationship between William I and William II and the Church. Include the reforms that William introduced and the disagreements that arose.

b Colour-code your timeline to show when the relationship was good and when it was bad.

c Write an account of the relationship between the Norman kings, William I, William II and the Church.

EXPLAIN

a Look back at your timeline. Circle the occasions in which the Papacy is mentioned.

b Explain what was important about William I and William II's relations with the Papacy.

CHAPTER 7

Monasticism

📖 **RECAP**

Monastic life

England's monasteries, abbeys and nunneries housed men and women who devoted their lives to Christianity. They followed a simple way of life laid down by the teachings of a religious leader. Under the Normans, St Benedict (c480–547) was the most influential holy teacher, giving his name to the Benedictine Order of **monasticism**.

Benedictine monks and nuns vowed to:

- give up all wealth and personal possessions (vow of poverty)
- abstain from sex and other physical pleasure, like alcohol and sweet food (vow of chastity)
- obey the teachings of God, as interpreted by their abbot or abbess (vow of obedience)
- never to leave their monastic community (vow of stability).

A day in the life of a monk or nun

- Monks and nuns lived away from the rest of society in order to avoid distractions and temptations.
- Monasteries and nunneries had to be totally self-sufficient, producing their own food and items for living. They would carry out most work themselves, but occasionally **lay** people (people who were not members of a religious order), who were not part of the order, were employed.
- Their day would often include the copying out of texts, tending to the sick or helping the poor.
- People could pay monasteries to pray for them, or their loved ones.

Timetable of a monk or nun	
00:00 First prayers of the day (Matins)	12:00 Church service (Sext); meal
03:00 Morning prayer (Lauds)	14:00 Rest
06:00 Get up; wash; church service (Prime)	15:00 Church service (None)
07:00 Meet for day's instructions	16:00 Farming and housekeeping
08:00 Private prayer and reading	18:00 Church service (Vespers)
09:00 Church service (Terce and Mass)	21:00 Night prayer (Compline); bed

Norman reforms of the monasteries

- William encouraged the building of abbeys and monasteries and many grand buildings were constructed.
- Abbots and abbesses were brought over from Normandy to ensure that the rules of St Benedict were being properly enforced.
- The Cluniac Order was introduced to England in 1077. It interpreted the Benedictine rules more strictly and was a more centralised system. This allowed for tighter control and made reform easier. There were 36 Cluniac monasteries in England by the end of the eleventh century.
- Under the feudal system, abbots could become rich landowners, but also had to provide knights to the king.
- William and his knights gave money to abbeys and monasteries as penance for the violent invasion.
- It became popular to send daughters who could not be married off and younger sons who would not inherit anything to become nuns and monks.

⚙ APPLY

INTERPRETATION ANALYSIS

Read the interpretation below.

▼ **INTERPRETATION A** *Adapted from an article on HistoryExtra.com, written by Marc Morris (2003):*

> The almost total replacement of the people at the top within a few years of 1066 had a major impact on the English church, for the newcomers had quite different ideas about the way the church should be governed… New attitudes were adopted: it was no longer acceptable for churchmen to buy their way into office, or to keep wives and mistresses. And new churches were built: laymen founded new monasteries, or refounded old ones, while bishops replaced their ancient cathedrals.

a Create a table with two columns. In the first column, copy out five key quotes from the interpretation. In the second column, write down whether your knowledge supports the statement being made. Be sure to include specific details.

b

> **EXAM QUESTION** How convincing is **Interpretation A** about the changes made to the Church by the Normans? Explain your answer based on your contextual knowledge and what it says in **Interpretation A**.

EXAMINER TIP

Remember to include specific facts in your answer from your contextual knowledge. You must go beyond the interpretation.

REVISION SKILLS

Memory maps or spider diagrams can be an excellent way of reviewing information. Use colours and small images to make the information memorable.

EXPLAIN

a Make a list of the duties performed by monks and nuns.

b Now make a list of the ways in which the existence of monasteries and nunneries benefited wider society.

c

> **EXAM QUESTION** Explain what was important about monasteries and nunneries in Norman times.

EXAMINER TIP

For an 'explain' question, you need to say why something is important, not just describe it.

REVIEW

You will need to look back at pages 50–53 to help you answer this question.

REVISION SKILLS

Reducing information to a shorter, more concise form is valuable. After reading a couple of pages of a textbook or your notes, ask yourself, 'what are the six most important things I need to remember?' Write those down on a piece of paper or small card. Don't worry about the things that you may have left out, you will remember those next time!

 **RECAP**

Schools and education

The challenges

- As the size and number of towns increased, a better education system was needed for the growing population.
- Improved literacy and numeracy skills were required in order for trade to be conducted.
- Norman barons and knights wanted their children to be educated to the highest level possible.
- Monastic reforms meant that children could no longer be educated within monasteries.

The changes under the Normans

- Schools moved out of religious grounds into separate buildings in towns and villages.
- A large number of new schools were established. By the twelfth century there were 40 schools and by the thirteenth century there were 75.
- French replaced the **vernacular** (local language of English) for teaching. All writing was done in Latin, the language of the Church.
- Archbishops Lanfranc and Anselm played a key role in the development of education in Norman England.
- One of the main functions of schools was to educate the clergy and produce literate lay people. Grammar schools were founded for this purpose.

The development of grammar schools

- At the age of ten, some wealthy boys were enrolled in grammar schools, where they would stay for at least four years. The length of time would depend on the career they intended to pursue.
- Girls did not attend school. Girls from richer families might be taught some reading and writing, perhaps by a tutor or by a parent, but it was rare.
- Students were taught to speak and write Latin, as well as a detailed understanding of Latin grammar.
- The school year began in September and there were three terms. The school year ended in June to allow peasant children to help with the harvest.
- The school day usually began at sunrise and lasted until late afternoon.
- After a school education, some students might go on to further study while others would begin jobs like parish priest, secretarial clerk or merchant.

SUMMARY

- Monasteries in England generally followed the teachings of St Benedict. This involved taking a series of vows to show their devotion to God.
- There were a number of developments in education under the Normans. These included an increase in the number of schools and the creation of grammar schools.
- Only boys had access to school.

 **APPLY**

WRITE AN ACCOUNT

a Create a mind-map showing the key developments in education under the Normans.

Schools moved out of religious grounds into separate buildings in towns and villages.

 Developments in education

b Make a set of flashcards summarising the changes to education under the Normans. You could use titles such as 'Students', 'Literacy', 'School Buildings', 'Uses for Education' and any others you can think of.

REVISION SKILLS

Making revision cards is a good way of revising and creating a useful revision aid for later use. Jot down three or four things under a heading on each card. Try to include a factual detail with each point.

EXPLAIN

a Make a list of the key features of the new grammar schools.

b For each item on your list, try to decide the reason for this feature. For example, students learned Latin because it was the language of the Church and also the language that all laws were written in.

c Why do you think the Normans introduced grammar schools?

d **EXAM QUESTION** Explain what was important about education in Norman England.

 EXAMINER TIP

In your answer you could consider how grammar schools helped to create a 'Norman society' to replace the Anglo-Saxon one that had existed before.

Exam practice

GCSE sample answers

 REVIEW

On these exam practice pages, you will find a sample student answer for each of the question types on the Norman England section of your Paper 2 exam. What are the strengths and weaknesses of the answers? Read the following pages and think carefully about what the student has written, what the examiner has said about each answer, and how you might improve your own answers.

The 'interpretation' question

▼ **INTERPRETATION C** *Adapted from* Ruling England, 1042–1217 (Second Edition) *by Richard Huscroft, published in 2016:*

> The English defensive line remained strong against Norman attacks until the feigned retreats began to weaken it. The decisions taken during the battle by Harold and William must have been crucial. William was a more experienced battlefield commander than his opponent. If the Norman accounts of Hastings are to be believed, he was both an inspirational leader capable of rallying his troops when they thought he was dead, and a tactical genius who saw the potential for victory in the chaos of the retreat of some of his soldiers.

EXAM QUESTION How convincing is **Interpretation C** about the reasons for William's victory at the Battle of Hastings? Explain your answer based on your contextual knowledge and what it says in **Interpretation C**. **8 marks**

Sample student answer

Interpretation C describes one of the major reasons for William's victory at the Battle of Hastings. It is convincing as the feigned retreats were indeed a major turning point in the battle.

Prior to the Norman soldiers' retreat, the Anglo-Saxon shield wall had been solid and, as the interpretation says, Norman attacks proved unable to break through the English line. The length of the battle suggests that the two sides were relatively equally matched despite the exhausted state of the Anglo-Saxon army.

Interpretation C is also convincing because it argues that William was a more experienced battlefield commander than Harold. Harold had fought a number of battles both before and after becoming king, but it is certainly true that William was more experienced. William's key advantage, however, was his ability to make quick tactical decisions in battle. Like other Norman commanders, William rode a horse into battle. This allowed him to move around the battlefield quickly, give orders and, most importantly, to rally his troops and show that he was still alive and in command. In contrast, Harold followed the Anglo-Saxon tradition of being on foot, among his men. While this may have raised the morale of those around Harold, it made effectively commanding his wider army more of a challenge.

EXAMINER TIP

The opening clearly states that the interpretation is convincing and shows the argument that will be made.

EXAMINER TIP

Additional detail could be added to explain why the Anglo-Saxon army was exhausted.

EXAMINER TIP

The use of the word 'convincing' relates directly to the question, and the contextual knowledge supports the point being made.

EXAMINER TIP

The interpretation refers to Norman accounts of the battle. This could be explored within the answer. How might it affect your view of the interpretation?

> William's victory at Hastings was the result of a number of factors, but his ability to make tactical changes and rally his troops when defeat seemed possible was certainly a key reason for the result.

EXAMINER TIP

This answer could be developed with more specific contextual knowledge, perhaps explaining some of the other reasons for William's victory.

OVERALL COMMENT

This answer is largely a Level 3 response. It gives a developed evaluation of the interpretation and includes a good level of contextual knowledge. It shows an understanding of more than one aspect of the interpretation. However, more knowledge would have moved the answer into Level 4.

OVER TO YOU

1 A big part of successfully answering an 'interpretation' question is showing a good level of contextual knowledge. This means including additional details about the events that the interpretation is describing. The key skill is knowing which bits of knowledge are relevant.

  a Use pages 24–25 to create a mind-map on the Battle of Hastings.

  b Now highlight the contextual knowledge on your mind-map that would be useful in answering this question.

2 Reread the first paragraph of the answer.

  a Write down two positive features and one area for improvement for this section.

  b Rewrite the paragraph incorporating your improvements.

3 Have a go at writing your own answer to the question (allow yourself a maximum of 10 minutes). When you have answered a question like this, ask yourself the following:

  a Have your shown that you understand the interpretation?

  b Have you said whether the interpretation fits with your knowledge of the period?

  c Have you made a judgement about whether it is 'convincing'?

The 'explain' question

 Explain what was important about the Church in Norman England.

8 marks

Sample student answer

One major way in which the Church was important in Norman England was its economic influence. Apart from the king, the Church was the biggest landowner in England. This gave many bishops significant secular power in addition to their power as Church leaders. Peasants on Church lands were required to work for free for a certain number of days a year. This took them away from working on their own lands. The Church also collected a tax known as a tithe. This was

EXAMINER TIP

Shows clear knowledge of the Church's role and includes specific facts.

ten per cent of everything produced by a farm in a year. In addition to tithes, William I agreed to honour the payment of Peter's Pence, a one penny tax on every household, paid to the Pope. The Church's wealth and its right to collect taxes made it incredibly powerful in Norman England.

 The Church was also important in Norman England because of its influence over all aspects of life. It was as important at the level of the parish priest among the peasants as it was among the king and the nobility. It also helped the Normans to control the Anglo-Saxons. The building of great cathedrals, as well as the Church's economic power made it a dominant force in people's lives and helped to make the country more Norman.

EXAMINER TIP

This answer would be improved if more was included about the role of the Papacy and its relationship with the English king, as well as other ways in which the Church influenced people's lives.

OVERALL COMMENT

This is a Level 3 answer. It includes a good level of contextual knowledge about the Church's importance and how it influenced the lives of ordinary people and those in power. In order to move into Level 4, the answer would need to include another area in which the Church was important and related to the wider context of changes in Norman England.

OVER TO YOU

1   How would you improve the sample answer?

   a   Highlight in one colour the key points at which the question is answered.

   b   Highlight in another colour anything that you think is not directly relevant to the question.

   c   Imagine you are an examiner: write down two strengths of this answer and two areas for improvement.

2   Now have a go at writing your own answer to the question using the sentence starters below. Allow yourself a maximum of 10 minutes to complete this task.

   The Church played an important role in Norman England...

   One reason for its importance was...

   A second reason was...

   Overall, it was important because...

3   Now check your answer:

   a   Have you explained what made the Church important?

   b   Have you included a range of detailed knowledge?

REVIEW

Before you tackle the question, take time to refresh your knowledge about the Church in this period by rereading pages 50–53

The 'write an account' question

 EXAM QUESTION Write an account of the ways in which law and order changed under the Normans.

Sample student answer

Following his invasion in 1066, William set about adapting the Anglo-Saxon system of law and order. Although many aspects stayed the same, there were a number of areas where changes were made.

One area of change was in the system of courts. Under the Anglo-Saxons, shire courts, which were overseen by the sheriff, met twice a year to consider cases on issues including land disputes and taxes. Although shire courts continued under the Normans, their importance declined. Under the Normans, hundred courts met more often and dealt with a wider range of issues.

Another area of change was inheritance. Under the Anglo-Saxons, it was common for land to be divided among the family when someone died. The Normans introduced the idea of primogeniture. This meant that all land was automatically passed onto the eldest son and that daughters and younger sons would inherit nothing. This ensured that earldoms remained intact, rather than being split after the death of the baron.

 EXAMINER TIP

A simple introduction addresses the question.

 EXAMINER TIP

Knowledge of the changes to courts is shown with specific details included.

 EXAMINER TIP

More specific detail about the wider context of these changes would improve this answer. Why did William introduce changes to law and order in England?

OVERALL COMMENT

This would be a Level 3 answer. It gives a number of examples of changes that the Normans made to law and order in England. It also demonstrates a good knowledge, although a wider knowledge of the period would have gained more marks.

OVER TO YOU

1 For this question, you need to show good knowledge of the changes made by the Normans. How well do you think the answer does this? Has anything been missed out?

2 Using the advice given here and your own feedback on the answer, rewrite the answer to improve it. Spend no more than 10 minutes doing this.

3 Now check your answer:

   a Have you included plenty of historical detail?

   b Have you shown a wider knowledge of the period?

The 'historic environment' question

 'One of the main reasons that the Normans built castles was to ensure control of the area.' How far does a study of Pevensey Castle support this statement? Explain your answer. You should refer to Pevensey Castle and your own contextual knowledge.

16 marks

Sample student answer

As soon as they arrived in England the Normans began building castles. Initially their aim was to secure the area that they had taken control of, as was the case at Pevensey, where the Normans first landed. This was where the first Norman castle was constructed. Castles also had a number of other purposes, all of which helped to maintain Norman control.

Castles acted as a clear message to the local population about who their new masters were and the power that they held. The size and speed with which castles could be constructed aimed to intimidate the Anglo-Saxons. Pevensey was a huge construction right in the heart of what had once been Harold Godwinson's earldom. It made it clear to the Anglo-Saxons that the Normans were here to stay.

The first castle built at Pevensey was a wooden structure brought from Normandy by William when he invaded. Pevensey was the southern gateway to Britain, and William's invasion had shown its vulnerability. The site of the castle had previously been the site of a Roman fort and William incorporated this into his new building. Like most Norman castles, the central feature of the original Pevensey castle was the motte: a mound of earth with the keep on top. The height allowed soldiers to see for miles and keep a lookout for threats. At Pevensey, the whole outer bailey was raised, so the motte was less obvious than elsewhere.

The strength of the castle meant that the area could be controlled with relatively few soldiers. Over time, Pevensey's wooden structure was replaced with a stone keep and strong stone walls. The design of castles, including Pevensey, had the aim of intimidating the local population, by showing the power of the Normans, and was therefore a very effective method of control.

One way in which castles helped maintain control was through location. Strategically, the location of Pevensey Castle was important for helping the Normans maintain control. It provided a good stopping point for travel between Normandy and England but also removed the risk of an invasion from the sea. Pevensey's importance was made clear in 1088 when there was an attempt to establish William's eldest son Robert Curthose as king, against his father's wishes. William's half-brother Robert of Mortain supported Robert, and William II was concerned that his brother would invade at Pevensey. William II ordered a siege of the castle, which lasted for six weeks until the occupants ran out of food. The castle was not successfully taken by force.

EXAMINER TIP

A clear and concise introduction that directly addresses the question.

EXAMINER TIP

More could be said about the specific features of Pevensey Castle.

EXAMINER TIP

Clear, specific detail about Pevensey to illustrate the wider point about castles.

The siege of 1088 demonstrates another vital purpose of castles: protection. Pevensey's thick outer bailey wall and heavily fortified gatehouse made it impossible for an attacker to take the castle. Normans were protected from the sometimes-hostile English.

Castles were designed to demonstrate the new hierarchy under the feudal system. The biggest and strongest part of the castle housed the Norman lord, while Anglo-Saxons lived at the bottom of the hill inside the bailey. The outer bailey included houses, workshops and, in hostile areas, places to keep livestock. The Anglo-Saxons within the bailey were therefore under the protection of the castle and its Norman guards. Castles like Pevensey became centres of trade and commerce, helping to establish the Norman way of life and instil long-term Norman control over England.

Overall, while castles like Pevensey were built for a number of reasons, the ultimate purpose was to establish Norman control over the area and the country as a whole. Castles achieved this in an obvious sense through their location and the soldiers that were stationed within, as well as the intimidation that they caused among the Anglo-Saxon peasants, but also in more subtle ways by reinforcing the hierarchy of the feudal system and becoming the centres of trade and commerce.

EXAMINER TIP

This point is not fully explained. How does trade and commerce help the Normans establish control over England?

EXAMINER TIP

A clear conclusion that summarises and answers the question.

EXAMINER TIP

However, the conclusion could be improved if it considered the wider context of castle building and Pevensey Castle itself during the Norman period.

OVERALL COMMENT

This is a Level 3 answer. It demonstrates a good knowledge of Norman castles in England. It could be improved by explaining more of the specific features of Pevensey Castle and their purpose.

OVER TO YOU

1. What are the strengths of this answer? Reread it and use a highlighter to identify its good elements.

2. What could be improved? Can you make any additions to the answer that would improve its quality?

3. Have a go at writing an answer to the question (allow yourself a maximum of 20 minutes). Once you have written an answer, ask yourself the following:

   a. Have you shown a good knowledge of the site, why it was built in the location and form that it was?

   b. Have you explained what it tells you about the period, linking it to your wider historical knowledge?

   c. Have you come to a clear conclusion that answers the question?

REVIEW

Look back at pages 28–29 to remind yourself about Norman castles and their purpose.

The answers provided here are examples, based on the information provided in the Recap sections of this Revision Guide. There may be other factors which are relevant to each question, and you should draw on as much of your own knowledge as possible to give detailed and precise answers. There are also many ways of answering exam questions (for example, of structuring an essay). However, these example answers should provide a good starting point.

Chapter 1 Page 13

WRITE AN ACCOUNT

a   Your spider diagram should include: government, population, society, defence, wealth and religion.

b   Answer might include: England was ruled by Edward the Confessor and was divided into smaller areas, controlled by earls. There was a clear hierarchy for society. England was a very wealthy country and was therefore often a target for foreign invaders, like the Vikings. Around 3000 housecarls, along with ordinary men, known as the fyrd, protected the country. However, there were few castles. There were strong trade links with other parts of Europe. Religion played a major part in the lives of English people, both as a guide to how to live your life and as a major landowner and legal authority.

EXPLAIN

a   A powerful family under after before Edward the Confessor. Earl Godwin was Earl of Wessex, his sons held other earldoms and his daughter was queen.

b   Answer might include:
  • They were powerful because of the positions they held and their popularity among English nobles and ordinary people.
  • They were powerful because Edward was unable to keep them in exile.
  • They were not that powerful because they relied on the king to maintain their position.
  • They were not that powerful because they were forced into exile in 1052.

Page 15

EXPLAIN

a   Your spider diagram should include:
  • The king's son – would have the strongest claim.
  • Another male relative – reasonable claim.
  • Male relative of a previous king.
  • King could name a successor to take over when he died (*post obitum*). If on his deathbed, known as *novissima verba*.
  • The Witan (leading earls and clergy) could nominate a successor.
  • Claimants could take the throne by force.

b   Answer might include:
  • **Harold Godwinson:** claimed he was promised the throne by Edward; supported by the Witan; supported by the majority of English earls.
  • **Edgar the Aetheling:** a blood relation (Edward's great-nephew).

c   Answer is likely to include:
  • Claim was strong because Harold Godwinson: had been promised the throne; was supported by the Witan and English nobles; was a member of the powerful Godwin family; served as sub-regulus; was the king's brother-in-law.
  • Claim was weak because he was not a blood relation.

WRITE AN ACCOUNT

a   Your fact file might include:
  • Following the death of his father, Earl Godwin, Harold had become 'sub-regulus', acting as a 'deputy king', from 1060 onwards.
  • He was Edward's brother-in-law.
  • He had shown loyalty to Edward, even over his own brother Tostig.
  • Harold claimed that Edward had promised him the throne on his deathbed.
  • He had the support of the English nobles and the Witan.
  • He had himself crowned king on 6 January, the same day as Edward's funeral.

b   Answer might include: Harold Godwinson believed he should be king for a number of reasons. He was England's most powerful earl, as Earl of Wessex and served as Edward's sub-regulus from 1060 onwards. Harold also claimed that Edward had promised him the throne on his deathbed. He had the support almost all of the English nobles and the powerful Witan.

Page 17

EXPLAIN

a   Your flashcards should use the information on pages 14 and 16. For Harold Godwinson, for example, you might write:
  • Named by the Witan.
  • Nominated by the previous king.

b   You might argue that Edgar had the strongest claim because he was a blood relation of Edward; or you might argue that Godwin had the strongest claim because he had the support of the Witan.

INTERPRETATION ANALYSIS

a   Answer might include:
  • The interpretation suggests that William's claim was based on propaganda. There is no evidence that Harold made an oath to support William's claim.

b   Answer might include:
  • The interpretation is convincing because it shows that William's claim was based on Harold's oath, and it questions whether this took place.
  • However, it is worth noting that there is conflicting evidence over whether the oath swearing actually took place.
  • It is convincing because it says that Edward may not have promised William the throne and it is true that there is no definitive evidence that he did.

Chapter 2 Page 19

WRITE AN ACCOUNT

a   You should produce your own flashcards from the spider diagram. These should include: the situation in France; getting across the channel; military preparations: building an army; military preparations: building a fleet and preparing to invade; the support of the Papal banner.

b Categorisation based on those suggested might include:

- Military: building of a fleet, army and ready-made castles.
- Political: security and stability in France, allowing William to leave Normandy.
- Religious: Papal Banner.

c Links might include:

- Papal Banner led to growth of the army.
- Political stability allowed William to focus on building a fleet.

d Answer might include:

- Details about William's preparations using information from the spider diagram.
- Categorisation and links between the preparations.
- An assessment of the importance of each aspect of William's preparations.

EXPLAIN

a Answer might include:

- The Papal Banner showed that William had the support of the Pope, and therefore God.
- It meant that more men were willing to join the fight.
- Less likely Normandy would be attacked while he was in England.

b It led to soldiers from outside Normandy joining his army and increasing his invasion force.

Page 21

WRITE AN ACCOUNT

a Storyboard should include Fulford Gate and Stamford Bridge.

b Answer might include:

- A description of events including Fulford Gate and Stamford Bridge.
- An assessment of the consequences: on the one hand, Harold has secured his throne from the Viking threat and killed a major rival, and on the other hand, Harold's men are exhausted and nearly 200 miles from the Norman invaders.

EXPLAIN

a List is likely to include: Edward's death, Harold's coronation, William's preparation, Harold's army being

disbanded, Hardrada's invasion, Fulford Gate, the march north, Stamford Bridge.

b Your timeline should show the events listed above.

c Events involving William might include his landing at Pevensey (28 September); for Godwinson you might include the Battle of Stamford Bridge (25 September); for Hardrada you might include the Battle of Fulford Gate (20 September)

Page 23

INTERPRETATION ANALYSIS

a **Anglo-Saxon army** = very large and well equipped.

Norman army = disorganised, 'a pack of curs'.

b Answer might include: Despite accounts at the time, the armies must have been evenly matched due to the length of the battle.

c Answer might include:

- It does fit because it suggested the armies were evenly balanced and they had a similar number of men.
- It does not fit because it suggests that William's men were disorganised, when in fact they were highly disciplined.

d Answer might include:

- It is convincing because it suggests that the two sides were evenly balanced.
- It is convincing because it says William's army had 'innumerable soldiers all well-equipped'. We know there were significant differences between the two armies and their weaponry. For example, William's army had archers and horses.
- The suggestion that William's men were disorganised and ill disciplined – 'a pack of curs' – could be challenged as William's discipline was harsh and his army was well equipped and organised.

EXPLAIN

a **William's advantages:** Experience; Papal Banner; number of soldiers; horses; weapons; soldiers were fresh and ready to fight.

Harold's advantages: On home soil; shield wall; good position on the battlefield with the advantage of height.

b Your answer needs to include specific reasons to justify your conclusion.

Page 25

WRITE AN ACCOUNT

a Your flow chart is likely to include: the shield wall, the feigned retreats, the Norman archers, and the death of Harold.

b Answer might include a narrative of the battle and an explanation as to why the outcome was as it was. Specific knowledge should be shown.

HISTORIC ENVIRONMENT

a You should produce your own flashcards.

b **Long term** might include: William's delay, Hardrada's invasion, the exhaustion of Harold's men.

Short term might include: feigned retreats, archers, Harold being on foot.

c You should be able to justify your order.

d Answer might include: the consideration of a number of factors in a battle, e.g. loser's mistakes, winner's strength/tactics and luck. This should be related to the specific example of the Battle of Hastings and include specific detail.

Chapter 3 Page 27

EXPLAIN

a Your spider diagram should include:

- Moved to Kent to secure ports in order to stop Anglo-Saxon trade and allow supplies to be brought in from Normandy.
- Strengthened his fortifications, building motte and bailey castles.
- Took control of Canterbury, the centre of the English Catholic Church.
- Burnt Southwark in retaliation for resistance in London.
- He secured Winchester, the base of the English treasury.
- At a meeting in Berkhamsted he insisted on an oath of loyalty from Edgar the Aetheling, Edwin and Morcar and leading nobles and bishops.

- He had himself crowned on Christmas Day, 1066 at Westminster Abbey.
- At the beginning of 1067, he began distributing land among loyal Norman barons as rewards and to ensure security and order.

b Examples might include:

Use of violence: Taking control of various towns; burning of Southwark.

No violence: Distributing land; castle building to intimidate the population.

a Your storyboard should include: William secures Kent and other ports; he builds motte and bailey castles; secures Canterbury and Winchester; burns Southwark; Forces Morcar, Edwin and Edgar to swear oaths of loyalty; crowned on Christmas Day 1066.

b Answer might include:
- A summary of William's actions and the events following the Battle of Hastings.
- An assessment of William's methods. Answer could be organised around violent methods (e.g. burning of Southwark, taking control of key towns) and political methods (e.g. distribution of land).

Page 29

HISTORIC ENVIRONMENT

a Key features might include: keep, bailey, motte, crenellations, moat/ditch.

b Reasons might include: control, hierarchy, intimidation, protection, administration.

c Answer should consider a number of reasons for building a castle (prompted by the mnemonic APICS). It should be related to the specific example of Pevensey Castle, the features of which can be directly linked to the reasons for its construction. Specific detail is needed. For example:
- Pevensey's location was symbolic of domination and control, as it was on the site of a Roman fort.
- It was rebuilt in stone and extended, suggesting permanence.
- It was part of a series of castles built in the area.

- It was a key location in terms of defence, trade and communication with Normandy.

EXPLAIN

a Answer is likely to include: an explanation as to why castles were built (APICS) placed in the context of early Norman England – i.e. the challenges that William faced during his reign.
- They were centres of administration.
- They offered protection for the Normans in the area, particularly the lord.
- They intimidated the local population and discouraged rebellion.
- They allowed the Normans to maintain control of an area without the use of a large army.
- They symbolised the new social structure: Normans at the top, English at the bottom.

Page 31

EXPLAIN

a Examples: 50 words: In 1075, William faced a rebellion from his own earls. It was led by Ralph de Gael and Roger de Breteuil and supported by the English earl, Waltheof, and the King of France. It was a serious threat but Odo and Lanfranc put it down. Most of the rebels were killed.

20 words: 1075 rebellion. Normans (Ralph de Gael and Roger de Breteuil) and English earl (Waltheof) defeated by Odo and Lanfranc. Serious threat.

10 words: 1075 Norman earls rebelled against William. Serious threat, but defeated.

b The revolt was led by Norman earls, whom William has appointed, whereas the others had all been Anglo-Saxons or, in the case of Eustace, a relative of Edward.

c Answer is likely to include:
- It was important because it represented a serious threat to William.
- It was important because it showed that even Norman earls could be a threat.
- It was important because it showed that William was able to deal with threats to his power.

WRITE AN ACCOUNT

a Your revision poster should cover:
- 1066 – Rebellion by Edwin and Morcar in London
- 1067 – Unrest along the Welsh border and in Hertfordshire
- 1068 – Rebellions in the south-west; Siege of Exeter by William; Harold Godwinson's sons land in Somerset
- 1069 – Second rebellion by the Welsh princes
- 1075 – Revolt of the Norman earls

b Answer is likely to include: An account of each rebellion and how it was dealt with. Make links between the rebellions and William's response.
- Rebellion of the Welsh border
- The Revolt of Eustace
- South West and Exeter
- Norman Earls
- Hereward the Wake.

Page 33

INTERPRETATION ANALYSIS

a Summary should include: William destroyed the lands, homes and livestock of the people in the north. By doing this it was responsible for the death of thousands of people.

b Answer is likely to include: Yes, because it describes the actions William took in devastating a huge area of the north of England.

c Answer is likely to include: It is convincing because it describes the actions William took. William ordered the burning of crops, the slaughter of livestock and the salting of the land to stop anything from growing.

WRITE AN ACCOUNT

a Your storyboard should include the causes, events and consequences.

b Answer might include:
- He wanted to show his power and to warn people not to rebel.
- He was angry at the number of rebellions that had taken place and wanted to put a stop to them once and for all.

c Answer is likely to include:

- Morcar, Edwin and Edgar fleeing north in 1068.
- King Malcolm giving support to Edgar.
- The murder of Robert of Commines and Bishop of Durham's house being set on fire.
- Edgar's attack on York.
- Danish support for Edward and the taking of York Castle.
- William's orders to devastate the north in response to the unrest.

Page 35

WRITE AN ACCOUNT

a You should make your own flowchart with a more detailed version of the following key points.

- Hereward launched a guerrilla campaign against the Normans.
- William put Hereward's base on the Isle of Ely under siege.
- A number of attempts were made to take the base.
- Eventually Hereward was betrayed by the monks in the abbey.

b Answer might include:

- It was different because it took the form of guerrilla-style attacks rather than a more straightforward uprising.
- It was different because it became more of a challenge for William to defeat.

c Answer is likely to include:

- Who Hereward was and why he rebelled.
- A description of the style of attack, perhaps with a reference to Peterborough.
- An account of the events at Ely, including William's three attempts to take the abbey.

EXPLAIN

a Common features include:

- It involved Anglo-Saxons who had lost out after William's invasion.
- Morcar played a role as he had in the first rebellion against William.

b Examples include:

- Edwin and Morcar rebelled in London shortly after the Battle of Hastings.
- Three of Harold Godwinson's sons landed on the Somerset coast in 1068.
- Waltheof joined the rebellion of the Norman earls.
- Edgar led an attack on York and seized the castle in the summer of 1069.
- Morcar was involved in the rebellion of Hereward the Wake.

c Answer might include:

- They were important because they were leading figures in a number of rebellions.
- They remained popular with ordinary English people who had supported Harold.
- They represented a challenge to William's throne.
- They were less important because the most serious rebellions required the support of Vikings or King Malcolm of Scotland, and were led by thegns rather than nobles (Edric and Hereward) or by Norman earls.

Chapter 4 Page 37

INTERPRETATION ANALYSIS

a Answer might include:

- The interpretation suggests that there was a huge change because the king and the barons had much more power under the Norman system.
- However, it also says that there was a development as William's changes took place within a system that already existed.

b Answer needs to give a reason.

c Answer might include:

- It is convincing because it says that there was some development of the Anglo-Saxon system. The structure was very similar with the king at the top, nobles underneath and the peasants at the bottom.
- It is also convincing because it says that the major change was that the king and barons were much more powerful than they had been under

the Anglo-Saxon system. William broke up some of the more powerful earldoms and established that all power ultimately belonged to him.

EXPLAIN

a Answer might include:

- It established that all land and power was William's and he could distribute it as he wished.
- It guaranteed loyalty from nobles because the king was free to take away their land.
- It provided an army for William when he needed it.
- It allowed him to replace Anglo-Saxons with Normans when the Anglo-Saxons rebelled against him.
- It provided William with wealth.

b Answer might include:

- It was important because it provided a clear structure and helped William to control England.
- It allowed him to reward those who had supported him in the past and ensured their future loyalty.
- It established Norman dominance over the Anglo-Saxons.

Page 39

EXPLAIN

a You should create your own mind-map.

b Answer might include:

- It shows who held land and wealth.
- It tells us the size of the population.
- It tells us the number of Norman settlers.
- It shows the extent to which Normans had replaced Anglo-Saxons as landholders.

c Answer is likely to include:

- It allowed William to see who held wealth, power and land in England.
- It showed him what taxes he could collect.

INTERPRETATION ANALYSIS

a William's changes were disastrous for the English aristocracy.

b Answer needs to refer to specific elements within the quotation and link to contextual knowledge.

c Answer is likely to include:

- It is convincing because it describes the impact of changes following the Norman invasion. It is true that, by the time of William's death, the vast majority of land was held by Normans.
- It is worth noting that after Hastings other Anglo-Saxon landholders who rebelled against William's rule lost their land when they were defeated.

Page 41
EXPLAIN

a Table is likely to include:

Continuity: shire and hundred courts continued; the ordeal system.

Change: changes to shire and hundred courts; establishment of primogeniture; introduction of murdrum fines; laws in Latin; ordeal by combat.

b Answer is likely to include: it was important because it maintained the structure that people were used to but slowly changed the system to follow the Norman approach to law and order. For example, the system of shire courts continued but, over time, hundred courts became more important.

WRITE AN ACCOUNT

a Answer might include:

- A description of the changes brought about by William I as shown in part a of the 'explain' question above.
- An analysis of whether law and order under William represented a continuation of the Anglo-Saxon system or a change from what had gone before.

Page 43
EXPLAIN

a Your timeline is llikely to include: William Rufus becoming king; disputed inheritance with Robert; rebellion in 1088; Anselm as Archbishop; Rufus' death.

b Timeline highlighted.

c Answer is likely to include:

- A narrative description of William Rufus's relationship with his brother

and the other events that led to his death.

- Some analysis of who could have been responsible, including who would have benefited from Rufus' death.

INTERPRETATION ANALYSIS

a Summary of the interpretation in your own words.

b Table might include:

Suspect: He had a disagreement with William; he refused to give the king money; he was loyal to the Pope; the king accused him of treason, which was punishable by death.

Not a suspect: It says that Anselm could not give money to the king because of his conscience. It seems unlikely his conscience would allow him to murder!

c Answer likely to include: It is convincing because it shows the disagreements the two men had over the Church; it shows William's temper, particularly his seemingly unreasonable accusation of treason.

Chapter 5 Page 45
WRITE AN ACCOUNT

a Annotations might include: The Church – important role of religion in daily life of peasants; the peasants' homes – usually cold and damp; the manor house – the home of the lord.

b Highlighted annotations showing examples of change and continuity.

c Answer might include:

- Daily life remained the same – the peasants worked long days in the fields and lived in the same homes.
- The Church remained powerful and the centre of village life.
- A local lord still controlled the area and the lives of the peasants.

EXPLAIN

a Lord, peasant, reeve, bailiff, priest, miller, craftsmen, servants.

b Suggestions might include:

- No priest = no marriages or wills.
- No miller = no bread for the village to eat.

Page 47
EXPLAIN

a Answer is likely to include: the establishment of guilds, the creation of markets and fairs, and specific examples of particular trades or industries leading to a town's growth, e.g. Droitwich and salt.

b Answer is likely to include: the importance of specific trades in towns that led to development. It might include reference to the importance of foreign trade, e.g. the wool trade, to coastal towns. It is also likely to explain the growing power and influence of guilds and the growth of markets and fairs.

WRITE AN ACCOUNT

a In addition to the role of trade, other branches might include: administration; control, and the Church.

b Answer is likely to include: some Anglo-Saxon towns declined while others became more important. For example, London and Norwich grew as important military centres, whereas Winchester became less important in this area, but more important as a religious centre. The answer is likely to describe changes including increase in trade, establishment of markets and fairs (by royal grant). There may be specific statistics from the Domesday Survey, e.g. 21 new towns developed between 1066 and 1100.

Page 49
INTERPRETATION ANALYSIS

a It suggests that while there were some very obvious changes, daily life may have changed very little.

b Outline your opinion and give reasons for it.

c Answer might include: It is convincing because it says that there were major changes like the building of castles and new laws, but it also recognises that, for many, life simply continued as it had before.

EXPLAIN

a Your list will include changes in relation to land (for example, earldoms were made much smaller), castles, law and language (for example, the new aristocracy spoke French).

b Answer is likely to include an outline of how the daily life of ordinary people changed under the Normans e.g. their work – still had to work for a lord, but a new one; new laws – forest laws and murdrum fines; and language – mainly English but some Norman words.

Chapter 6 Page 51

HISTORIC ENVIRONMENT

a Features will include: Romanesque style, rounded arches, vaulted ceilings, building in shape of a cross, quires, symmetrical design.

b Answer is likely to include: A description of the key features of Durham Cathedral and an explanation as to how these features reflect its purpose. The answer is likely to consider how far the cathedral was the result of religious devotion and how far it reflects other aims, e.g. intimidating the population and establishing control.

EXPLAIN

a You should produce your own flashcards showing changes.

b The order will be your own.

c Answer is likely to outline the main features of the Norman Church and its influence on the lives of people in England. For example:
  • It guided people about how to live their lives in a godly way.
  • It collected taxes in the form of tithes.
  • It conducted baptisms, marriages and funerals.
  • It owned land and peasants were expected to work it for free.

Page 53

WRITE AN ACCOUNT

a You should produce your own timeline showing key developments.

b The colour-coding will be your own.

c Answer is likely to include an outline of the key developments in the relationship including: William I's and Lanfranc's reforms; monastic changes; cathedrals; reforms and the role of Anselm; William II and the Papacy.

EXPLAIN

a You will make your own choices.

b Answer is likely to include an outline of the key developments in the relationship including: papal support for William I's invasion; Peter's Pence; disagreements over reform (Anselm).

Chapter 7 Page 55

INTERPRETATION ANALYSIS

a Table should include five quotes with a link to contextual knowledge.

b Answer is likely to include: It is convincing because it explains the reforms introduced by the Normans to cut down on the amount of corruption. At Durham Cathedral, Benedictine monks were introduced by William of St Calais because they could be depended on to follow their vows.

EXPLAIN

a List should include: prayer, helping the sick, domestic chores, farming.

b Answer might include:
  • Treating the sick.
  • Praying for people and their relatives (for a fee).
  • Providing an option for families with a daughter without a husband or for a younger son without an inheritance.

c Answer might include:
  • They provided prayers and health care for people.
  • They provided an option for families with a daughter without a husband or for a younger son without an inheritance.
  • They allowed the nobility to pay penance by giving them money.
  • They gave power to abbots as land owners under the feudal system.

Page 57

WRITE AN ACCOUNT

a Mind-map should include:
  • Schools moved out of religious grounds into separate buildings in towns and villages.
  • A large number of new schools were established.
  • French replaced the vernacular (English) for teaching. All writing was done in Latin, the language of the Church.
  • Archbishops Lanfranc and Anselm played a key role in the development of education.
  • One of the main functions of schools was to educate the clergy and grammar schools aimed to produce literate lay people.

b You should make your own flashcards showing changes.

EXPLAIN

a • Some wealthy boys were enrolled in grammar schools, where they would stay for at least four years.
  • Girls did not attend school.
  • Students were taught to speak and write Latin.
  • The school year began in September and there were three terms.
  • The school year ended in June to allow peasant children to help with the harvest.
  • The school day usually began at sunrise and lasted until late afternoon.

b Answer must justify each feature. An example could be: School year runs from September to June to allow peasant children to help with the harvest.

c Answer might include:
  • To increase the level of education among ordinary people in order to boost trade.
  • To make people feel 'Norman' and further establish William's control.

d Answer is likely to include similar points to question c. It will likely expand on these points.

aetheling of noble birth

bailey an encircled area of land around, or at the base of, a motte

baron a person at the lower end of the nobility who held land from the king

burgess urban (town) dweller

celibate to refrain from sex or physical pleasure

clergy members of a religious order, e.g. priests

demesne all the land owned by a particular lord

doom painting a large painting in a church that shows images of heaven and hell

earl a member of the nobility

fallow a field that is left empty for a year or two to give the soil time to recover

feigned retreat pretending to run away

freeman peasant who paid rent to the lord instead of loyalty

fyrd a medieval army made up of peasants

grant a sum of money given by a government

guerrilla a type of warfare where soldiers fight in small groups and hide in order to catch out the enemy

guild an organisation of craftsmen and merchants from a specific craft or industry

Holy War a war fought either on behalf of God or with the support of God

honorial court often in castles; where tenants could appeal against their landlord

housecarl professional well-trained soldier hired by the king or an earl

hundred a subdivision of an Anglo-Saxon shire, which was 100 hides in size (a hide is c120 acres)

minting the process of making coins

monasticism a religious way of life in which one renounces worldly pursuits to devote oneself fully to spiritual work

motte a mound, either manmade or natural; in Norman times, utilised for castle building

murdrum fine the heavy fine payable to the king by an entire area where the criminal lived if a Norman earl was murdered

novissima verba to be promised the throne from a death bed

Papal Banner formal support given by the Pope to a king

patronage land, titles or power given to ensure an individual's support

pluralism to hold more than one position in the Church

post obitum a designation or bequest of a throne

primogeniture process by which the eldest son inherited all the land or titles from his father; younger sons or daughters would be left with nothing

propaganda deliberately chosen information presented in order to influence people to think something specific

Romanesque style of architecture common in Europe from the tenth to the twelfth century

scutage tax paid to the monarch instead of service

sheriff the kings' chief legal official in an area

shrine a place or casket associated with a saint

subinfeudation the splitting of land with a social inferior by a lord who expected homage in return

sub-regulus deputy king

tenant-in-chief someone who held land from the king

thegn a person who owned land but was not a noble

vernacular local language spoken by ordinary people

villein a peasant

Witan a group of leading earls and churchmen

Notes

Topics available from *Oxford AQA GCSE History*

Student Books and Kerboodle Books

Paper One: understanding the modern world

Period Study

Germany 1890–1945 Democracy and Dictatorship
Student Book
978 019 837010 9
Kerboodle Book
978 019 837014 7

America 1920–1973 Opportunity and Inequality
Student Book
978 019 841262 5
Kerboodle Book
978 019 841263 2

Wider World Depth Study

Conflict and Tension: The Inter-War Years 1918–1939
Student Book
978 0 19 837011 6
Kerboodle Book
978 019 837015 4

Conflict and Tension between East and West 1945–1972
Student Book
978 019 841266 3
Kerboodle Book
978 019 841267 0

Conflict and Tension in Asia 1950–1975
Student Book
978 019 841264 9
Kerboodle Book
978 019 841265 6

Conflict and Tension: First World War 1894–1918
Student Book
978 019 842900 5
Kerboodle Book
978 019 842901 2

Paper Two: Shaping the nation

Thematic Study

Thematic Studies c790–Present Day
Student Book
978 019 837013 0
Kerboodle Book
978 019 837017 8

Contents include **all 3 Thematic Study options:** Health, Power, and Migration, Empires and the People

British Depth Study

British Depth Studies c1066–1685
Student Book
978 019 837012 3
Kerboodle Book
978 019 837016 1

Contents include **all 4 British Depth Study options:** Norman, Medieval, Elizabethan, and Restoration England

---

Covering all 16 options

Teacher Handbook

Teacher Handbook
978 019 837018 5

Kerboodle Exam Practice and Revision

Kerboodle Exam Practice and Revision
978 019 837019 2

Revision Guides 📖 RECAP ⚙ APPLY ↻ REVIEW ✓ SUCCEED

Germany 1890–1945 Democracy and Dictatorship
Revision Guide: 978 019 842289 1
Kindle edition: 978 019 842290 7

America 1920–1973 Opportunity and Inequality
Revision Guide: 978 019 843282 1
Kindle edition: 978 019 843283 8

Conflict and Tension: The Inter-War Years 1918–1939
Revision Guide: 978 019 842291 4
Kindle edition: 978 019 842292 1

Conflict and Tension between East and West 1945–1972
Revision Guide: 978 019 843288 3
Kindle edition: 978 019 843289 0

Conflict and Tension in Asia 1950–1975
Revision Guide: 978 019 843286 9
Kindle edition: 978 019 843287 6

Britain: Power and the People c1170–Present Day
Revision Guide: 978 019 843290 6
Kindle edition: 978 019 843291 3

Health and the People c1000–Present Day
Revision Guide: 978 019 842295 2
Kindle edition: 978 019 842296 9

Norman England c1066–c1100
Revision Guide: 978 019 843284 5
Kindle edition: 978 019 843285 2

Elizabethan England c1568–1603
Revision Guide: 978 019 842293 8
Kindle edition: 978 019 842294 5
